DAVE WILLIAMS

HOPE
IN THE
LAST
DAYS

FRONT
LINE

Most CHARISMA HOUSE BOOK GROUP products are available at special quantity discounts for bulk purchase for sales promotions, premiums, fund-raising, and educational needs. For details, write Charisma House Book Group, 600 Rinehart Road, Lake Mary, Florida 32746, or telephone (407) 333-0600.

HOPE IN THE LAST DAYS by Dave Williams
Published by FrontLine
Charisma Media/Charisma House Book Group
600 Rinehart Road
Lake Mary, Florida 32746
www.charismahouse.com

This book belongs in the collection of every pastor who wants to teach his or her members about the last days. Dave cuts right to the chase on what you need to do to understand the coming events foretold by the ancient prophets. Get prepared and filled with hope as you read this book. A must-read for anyone who wants to understand Bible prophecy.

—Pastor Matthew Barnett
CEO of The Dream Center
Los Angeles, California
www.dreamcenter.org

Brimming with hope, this book gives powerful, practical, and solid advice on preparing for the last days. Read it and you'll be glad you did. Dave Williams is truly one of America's great leaders.

—Pastor Tommy Barnett
Founder of Los Angeles Dream Center &
Phoenix Dream Center
Phoenix, Arizona
www.dreamcitychurch.us

What a treasured resource this book is—absolutely amazing! Dave Williams has the ability to unpack end-time prophetic events unlike anyone I have ever known. Love it!

—Rev. Kevin Berry
Pastor, Mount Hope Church
Lansing, Michigan
www.mounthopechurch.org

Dave Williams has once again provided a fantastic book that will equip pastors, believers, and leaders to teach on biblical prophecy with confidence. This book is biblically sound and contains a vital message for the church today. It should be in every pastor's library.

—Pastor Richard Crisco
Rochester Christian Church
Rochester, Michigan
www.RCChurchlife.org

Dave Williams masterfully handles the controversial subject of the end times, giving us hope for our future as believers in Christ. I am personally challenged for global evangelism even more as a result of this impactful book. This is an urgent must-read for every believer.

—Rev. Jennifer Eivaz
Author of *The Intercessors Handbook*
Turlock, California
www.jennifereivaz.com

In *Hope in the Last Days* Dr. Dave Williams gives us a balanced and refreshing look into God's promise of the last days. In every significant revival, hope for the imminent return of Christ has played a central role. As you read Dave Williams's latest book, you will experience the stirring of the Holy Spirit as you look with hope to the coming of our precious Jesus!

—Rev. Ron Eivaz
Pastor, Harvest Christian Center
Turlock, California
www.harvestturlock.org

Dave is a no-nonsense individual who doesn't deal in hopelessness. This book deals straightforwardly with the reality of end-time events, but its chief objective is to fill us with hope and move the Christian to action. Dave encourages us to remember our future is as bright as all the promises of God.

—Rev. John Gunn
Executive Director of The Power Company Kids Club
Pontiac, Michigan
www.powercompanykidsclub.org

Thank you, Dave Williams, for an incredible Bible-based account of the last days. I am stirred, moved in my spirit, and thankful that we do have hope in the end times! This book is a culmination of a lifetime of study, research, history, inspiration, and anointing to give us hope in the days to come!

—Big John Hall
Classic Inspirational Gospel Music Singer
Fort Worth, Texas
www.bigjohnhall.com

Dave Williams has done it again! No one does a better job at making the often complex and confusing subject of end-time events simple to understand. Dave's straightforward teaching is clear and full of hope, and it brings great joy to believers! In these days this is a must-read for every Christian.

—Rev. Beth Jones
Author of *Getting a Grip on the Basics*
Portage, Michigan
www.bethjones.org

Dr. Dave Williams is a phenomenal and gifted communicator of the truths of God's Word. He is able to make the most complicated subjects easy to comprehend. His latest work, *Hope in the Last Days*, is just another example of this amazing gift as it brings hope for the days ahead. It will be hard to put this book down once you begin reading it.

—Rev. Jeff Jones
Pastor, Valley Family Church
Kalamazoo, Michigan
www.valleyfamilychurch.org

Wow—what a great book! Dave Williams cuts right to the chase on what you need to know to understand the coming events foretold by the ancient prophets. This should be required reading for every church leader. Thanks, Dave—you've made an incredible contribution to the church in these last days.

—Rev. Bill Leach
Former Assemblies of God Superintendent,
Michigan District
Farmington Hills, Michigan

Any astute believer has to recognize that we are viewing the end of time from a front-row seat. *Hope in the Last Days* by my friend Dave Williams offers a concise, authentic, and complete handbook to teach and help us navigate these turbulent waters, always remembering the operative word—*HOPE!*

—Rev. Arthelene Rippy
Television Personality, Christian Television Network
Clearwater, Florida
www.ctnonline.com/homekeepers

Dr. Dave Williams is one of the finest men we have ever known. He has a heart for God's people and trust in his heavenly Father, and his understanding of the scriptures about the last days is so profound and yet so easy to understand and comprehend. His leadership is unprecedented, and his ability to unfold the scriptures from the Book of Revelation is powerful and insightful. Don't miss this opportunity to go deeper and higher all at the same time as you dive into *Hope in the Last Days!*

—Harry and Cheryl Salem
Cofounders and President
Salem Family Ministries
Cathedral City, California
www.salemfamilyministries.org

Dave Williams has always had a clear grasp of the end times. He's preached and taught about it since the 1970s. This book highlights the last "hours" in which we live. In bringing understanding of the prophetic messages in the Bible, Dave brings hope to the reader.

—Rev. Clarence St. John
Assemblies of God Superintendent,
Minnesota District
Minneapolis, Minnesota
www.mnaog.org

Cover design by Vincent Pirozzi
Design director: Justin Evans
Charts by Kristy Grundner

Visit the author's website at www.davewilliams.com.

Library of Congress Cataloging-in-Publication Data:
An application to register this book for cataloging has been submitted
to the Library of Congress.
International Standard Book Number: 978-1-62998-939-6
E-book ISBN: 978-1-62998-940-2

17 18 19 20 21 — 9 8 7 6 5 4 3 2 1
Printed in the United States of America

*This book is dedicated to the faithful pastors
who are still preaching "Jesus is coming!"*

CONTENTS

Acknowledgments... xiii

Foreword *by Dr. Jack Van Impe* xv

Introduction xvii

1 **History Converges: The Times and the Seasons**.................. 1

    The Times in Which We Live....................................... 2

    Date Setters 6

    Prophecy Brings Hope.. 8

    Sealed Prophecies 10

    God Is a God of Order 12

2 **Avoiding Prophetic Pitfalls and**
   Defining Eschatological Terms 14

    Some Will Miss Their Hour of Visitation 14

    Defining Prophetic Terms....................................... 16

    Caution Against Sloppy Eschatology............................. 22

    A Few Sensible Rules for Understanding Prophecy................. 26

    You *Can* Understand Bible Prophecy! 28

3 **The Spirit of Prophecy:**
   How I Personally Met Jesus in Bible Prophecy.................. 29

    How I Met Jesus in Daniel 2..................................... 30

    Sneaking Up to the Radar Room 31

    Daniel's Background 32

    A Prophecy for Then and Now 33

    Prophecy Brought Me to Jesus................................... 37

4 **The Prophetic Chronology:**
   Nothing Makes Sense Without This 39

    Prophetic Order 39

The Seventy Weeks and the Missing Seven Years 41

The Prince Who Shall Come 45

The Coming Imposter 47

Something Global, Dramatic, and Irreversible 47

The General Prophetic Chronology of End-Time Events 49

An Exciting Project. 53

Decoding the Apocalypse 54

5   Preview Signs of the Apocalypse:
A Sneak Peek Into the Future 57

Don't Ignore the Signals 57

Preview Signs. 59

Blinkers and Lights 60

Beheadings. 60

Water Contamination 61

Euphrates River Drying Up 61

Violence. 62

Famines, Epidemics, and Earthquakes 63

Wars and Rumors of War 64

The Sign of Israel Blinks Strong 65

Silence and Darkness. 66

Unresolvable National Problems 67

Attacks on the Truth 68

6   Last Days Nations and Groups:
The Chilling Accuracy of the Ancient Prophets 73

Israel 73

European Nations. 75

Magog Nations. 80

The Spectator Nations That Question the Invasion 84

Terrorist Groups 86

Terrorists Terrorized and Neutralized 89

Syria. 90

Elam. 91

Islam Is Approaching Its Demise 91

China 93

**7   The United States in Bible Prophecy:
    What the Future Holds for This Superpower 97**

A Village of Tarshish?. 97

The Eagle of Revelation 12? 98

The New Babylon? 99

Sudden and Dramatic Decline 101

America Has Been Warned 103

Two Pillars of the United States 106

A Better Possibility 109

**8   The Mystery Nation:
    You Carry the Power of Another World 111**

Mysteries in the Bible 112

Agents of Another World 114

The Lost in Need of Hope 115

A Season of Revival 116

Opening Blind Eyes 118

Conflicting Prophecies? 119

Praying Like Priests 120

A Special Mark of Protection for Intercessors. 121

Prayers Will be Answered in the Tribulation 122

Ambassadors Speak What Their King Speaks. 123

An Imam Joins the Mystery Nation 124

Reaching One Hundred Thousand 126

Ambassadors Called Home 127

**9   The Great Secret Revealed:
    The Mystery of the Disappearance of Millions. 128**

Two Trumpets. 130

Marriage Supper 132

Aftermath on Earth 134

Dealing With Israel 135

Different Views of When 136

Encroachment on the Doctrine of Imminence 138

Third Day Theory 143

10   The Final *Shabua*:
Earth's Inescapable Hour of Agony and Distress 145

A New Global Leader Arises 145

Days of Noah 151

The Mask Comes Off 153

Trapped on Earth 154

Unrepentant People 156

America Stands By, Helpless................................... 157

Russia and Iran Invade 158

What to Do If You Miss God's Final Roundup—the Rapture........ 159

11   The Coming Kingdom: After Jesus Returns.................... 165

The Real King Is Back... 167

The First Seventy-Five Days 168

Those Who Survive the Final *Shabua* 168

The End of the Millennium 171

The Earth Is Recommissioned.................................. 172

12   Final Words: Admonitions and Encouragement 174

Defectors From the Faith 174

The First Three Things I Look for in a Church................. 175

Defend Against Deception 178

Preparing for the Final Hours................................ 179

Appendix
How to Ask Jesus to Be Your Savior and
Become a Part of His Kingdom............................... 181

Notes... 183

Bibliography... 199

ACKNOWLEDGMENTS

I WISH TO GIVE a very special thanks to the wonderful folks who have helped me with this project:

First, to my precious wife, Mary Jo, who has served as my chief intercessor for nearly forty years and assisted me in making sure each chapter was readable.

Next, to my dear friends, Drs. Jack and Rexella Van Impe, who have spoken into my life for many years and invested much time with me personally.

To Joel Kilpatrick, who is a remarkable writer and "pruner"; Robert Glennon, my executive director; Kristy Grundner, my graphics designer and diagram maker; Linda Teagan, director of our print media ministry; and Maureen Eha, Kimberly Overcast, Adrienne Gaines, and the entire Charisma Media team, who are great to work with.

I also want to thank Dr. Ed Hindson, Dr. Mark Hitchcock, Dr. Ron Rhodes, Dr. David Reagan, and author Bill Salus, who relentlessly continue to research and present their prophetic findings. These men have been a great influence on me.

FOREWORD

OVER TWENTY YEARS ago I met Dr. Dave Williams when Rexella and I spoke at his Bible institute's graduation in Lansing, Michigan. Since then we have shared many times together, both formal and informal.

I'll never forget the night I preached at Mount Hope Church where Dave was pastoring. Seven thousand people came to hear me teach on Bible prophecy. Under Dave's leadership, the church had planted several daughter churches, which were connected that night by satellite. The three-thousand-seat sanctuary was full as well as every overflow area in the building, the chapel, and the event center; television monitors were set up even in the foyer so everyone could be a part of the service. That night was like another Pentecost, because more than three thousand people came to Jesus Christ as I gave the invitation (Acts 2:41). This type of response was not only happening in Lansing but also at all the participating churches connected by satellite.

Rexella and I were honored and encouraged to find a pastor of a large ministry who was teaching Bible prophecy to his flock. (In fact, Dave even admitted to preaching my sermon years ago on Ezekiel 38 and 39!) It was good to see a pastor who loved evangelism, took the Bible literally, and believed that Jesus is coming soon.

The Bible warns that some will depart from the faith in the last days (1 Tim. 4:1). It's always a blessing to know a pastor who sticks with the Bible, God's Word. I love it when pastors teach about prophecy. Prophecy is not difficult to understand when you learn the simple rules of prophetic interpretation.

When I was in the hospital at death's door not long ago, I trusted

Dave to fill in for me four times on our global telecast. I know he has a heart for pastors who want to understand and teach Bible prophecy.

I have been writing books and recording messages about Bible prophecy (eschatology) for nearly seventy years to promote discernment among believers and to bring the unsaved to Jesus Christ. And now, may God bless you as Dr. Dave Williams presents *Hope in the Last Days*.

—Dr. Jack Van Impe
Host, *Jack Van Impe Presents*

INTRODUCTION

WE SEEM TO be approaching eternity at breakneck speed.

We live in the very first generation to see all the end-time signs converging. No other generation has witnessed such a massive stage-setting time as this. Jesus instructed His followers to look up when we see "these things," for this generation will not pass before the fulfillment of "all these things" (Luke 21:28, 32).

The apocalyptic storm clouds foretold by the ancient biblical prophets are now arriving. The hearts of people everywhere hunger to know the future. *Hope in the Last Days* will walk you through the end-time prophecies, helping you prepare for what is about to transpire on the earth.

Renowned scientist Sir Isaac Newton, who was also an avid researcher of biblical apocalyptic prophecy, said, "About the Time of the End, a body of men will be raised up who will turn their attention to the Prophecies, and insist upon their literal interpretation, in the midst of much clamor and opposition."[1]

Church sermons on Bible prophecy are rare these days. My prayer is that God will use this book to provide pastors with a clear understanding of the apocalyptic timeline, and that they will in turn help their congregations understand prophecy. Global and dramatic events are on the horizon, and God's people must be equipped, like the sons of Issachar, to understand the times (1 Chron. 12:32).

Prophecy is sort of like a jigsaw puzzle. You begin by getting all the pieces of the border in place before you begin connecting the other pieces. When you assemble the border first, it's much easier to find, little by little, where the remaining pieces of the puzzle fit. This book is designed to give you the borders.

It is more than a prophecy study, however. It's about you, your family, and your future, so share it with your loved ones. My sincere prayer is that *Hope in the Last Days* will lead you, your family, your church, and your workplace into deeper, more fruitful fellowship with Jesus Christ.

Let's begin our adventure into the days ahead.

Chapter 1

HISTORY CONVERGES

THE TIMES AND THE SEASONS

I will come again.
—JESUS, JOHN 14:3

JUST AS THE ancient prophets predicted, nations are aligning and prophetic warnings are rapidly converging. Evidence is mounting up all around us, making it clear that we are living in the last days of this world as we know it.

People of all religious backgrounds are showing tremendous and uncanny interest in apocalyptic prophecy today. They have a sense that the stage is being set for the final events of this age. Everyone is asking, "What will the future bring? How can we know for sure?"

Hollywood exploits our desire to know the future. The past decade has brought more apocalyptic films and stories to the public than at any other time in history. You can feel an excitement in the air, coupled with an eerie foreboding about the events just beginning to unfold.

Something dramatic, global, and irreversible lies just ahead. There is no way to avoid it. The stage is set and the actors are in place, preparing to follow their script for what will shortly transpire on the earth.

Can we understand what is coming to this world? Are Hollywood's "prophecies" the best insight we have into our times? Or can we see more clearly and know in advance what is coming so we can prepare ourselves? The answer is yes, we can! We have a better answer. It is found in God's prophetic timeline and the signs He gave us. These were written down plainly in God's Word.

Prophecies are not spooky or mysterious pronouncements with understanding reserved only for an exclusive few. Prophecy is a gift from God for all of humanity—a glimpse, and sometimes more than a glimpse, of what lies ahead, perhaps in our own lifetimes. When we ignore it, we turn our backs on the only sure record of the future that exists in our world today. What you believe about prophecy will dramatically affect your future, the way you live your life, and how you prepare for what lies ahead.

Are you ready? Our generation is racing toward the hour spoken of by the ancient biblical prophets called the "day of the Lord" (Joel 2:31; Acts 2:20) or "the hour of temptation that shall come upon the entire world" (Rev. 3:10).

Prophecy researchers today are suggesting that New Age leaders are predicting the unfolding of "Earth's hour of cleansing," a time when those "not of Earth's harmony" will be taken from this planet.[1] Are they preparing the minds of their followers for what is about to transpire?

Eternity is indeed approaching us at great speed as the prophetic signs become more frequent and increasingly intense. Just ahead the world will experience shocking events that will eclipse anything ever recorded in history. If you thought the past was intense, get ready for the future.

The Times in Which We Live

Today the daily headlines seem to scream in unison, "It won't be long now." Something is going to happen that will shake the nations. That "something" will be sudden, dramatic, and irreversible.

One headline recently blared, "World War III Has Begun."[2] Another news report was titled "Pope Francis: World War III Has Begun—Third Secret of Fatima Gives Warning."[3] We know from Scripture that World War III will occur in phases, the first beginning in the Middle East. (See Psalm 83; Isaiah 17; Jeremiah 49;

Ezekiel 38–39.) It shouldn't pass without notice that Russia has been providing Hezbollah, a terrorist military group operating in Lebanon, with advanced military weapons, including laser-guided rockets and long-range tactical missiles, without any restrictions with regard to attacking Israel.[4] In March 2016 a news article reported that Hezbollah was preparing for the "biggest war ever" with Israel.[5]

War is not just breaking out in the Middle East. The world mourned as we watched the horrors unfold in Paris in 2015 when Islamic gunmen and suicide bombers attacked the Bataclan concert hall. These jihadists also targeted innocent people at a stadium, restaurants, and bars, and before the attacks ended, 130 people were dead and hundreds were wounded.

Imagine being trapped in a building with terrorists shouting, *"Allahu akbar,"* and systematically murdering concertgoers one by one, or being a parent, knowing your son or daughter is trapped in the concert hall as you watch the news. The horror is unimaginable. As Shepard Smith of Fox News whispered while covering the incident, "We are in a new world, with a new future, and all the things we've planned have changed."[6]

Some people see everything as a sign. Others see nothing as a sign. We must avoid both extremes. But signs are important. What if there were no stop signs? Street signs? Speed limit signs? High voltage signs? These types of signs serve to maintain order and prevent chaos. Prophetic signs are even more important. And they are popping up all over, pointing to the soon return of Jesus Christ. You are either ready or you are not—it's that simple. Prophetic signs are like "previews of coming attractions." They are not the main attraction, but they point to it. Signs provide small glimpses of what the main feature will be like.

I first began my studies in Bible prophecy in November 1971. By 1978 I understood and publicly taught that in the final hours of the last days certain signs would become increasingly evident:

   1. The world's focus would be on the Middle East.

2. Russia would begin to align with key Muslim nations.

3. Israel would be surrounded by those bent on its annihilation.

4. Anti-Semitism would dramatically escalate.

5. Religious deception would be rampant.

6. Political chaos would increase, and a political star with plausible solutions would rise up.

7. Extreme famines would occur in different parts of the world.

8. There would be wars and rumors of war, especially relative to the Middle East and Israel.

9. Epidemics and pandemics would spread.

10. Earthquakes and natural disasters would escalate in frequency and intensity.

11. Technology would advance in astonishing ways.

12. Terrorism would jump to the forefront.

13. There would be an abnormal emphasis on sex and materialism, and morality would be twisted.

14. Betrayals, multiplying family problems, and resistance to God's messages would be prevalent.

15. A genuine, Holy Spirit–led revival would emerge as a remnant of godly believers would place their focus on the Lord Jesus Christ and His power.

Those signs are now joining together at whirlwind velocity. But much like an alarm clock, many choose to ignore it. Signs can be agitating, discomforting. Somehow we want to believe, *Maybe we still have a few years or decades before these prophecies come to pass.* But the evidence tells us they are upon us now. The Day of the Lord truly will come—any day! Jesus promised, "So also, when you shall see all these things, you know that it is near, even at the doors. Truly I say to you, this generation will not pass away until all these things take place" (Matt. 24:33–34). The generation that sees these signs taking place simultaneously and globally will be part of the final generation, and they will possibly experience the long-awaited return of Jesus Christ. While followers of Christ will walk in hope, faith, and great power, others will taste only anguish and distress in the days ahead.

This book is designed to help you and your family prepare with hope for the end of this age, not as "preppers," but as hope-filled, faith-drenched followers of Jesus Christ with ears tuned to what the Holy Spirit is saying (Rev. 2:7).

Tragically many Christians today no longer even know what they believe about Bible prophecy. This is largely due to three reasons:

1. A number of pastors are not teaching prophecy.

2. There have been many false alarms in the past few decades.

3. Unqualified teachers offer sincere but faulty opinions.

The doctrine of the imminent coming of Christ for His church was once the bright and blessed hope of the church (Titus 2:13). *Imminent* means "inevitable, looming, may occur at any moment," and Christians actually believed that at any moment Christ could take them to heaven.

Today the doctrine of imminence has often become the target of ridicule and jokes from the "more intellectual scholars" who pity those who still believe that Christ is coming for them. Replacement theologians argue that those who teach and believe the doctrine of imminence are teaching simple escapism. Yet it was Jesus Himself who instructed His followers to "watch always and pray that you may be counted worthy to escape all these things that will happen" (Luke 21:36).

Local pastors rarely preach regular sermons on biblical prophecy anymore. And because of this neglect, many people in our churches have become prophetically illiterate, open to all kinds of aberrant and error-riddled prophetic teachings.

Pastors who do teach Bible prophecy are enjoying surprising growth in their congregations today, just as Calvary Chapel did during the Jesus movement. Pastor Chuck Smith most likely did not have every detail of prophecy precisely correct. Yet he taught it regularly, and the Costa Mesa church grew from twenty-five to more than twenty-five thousand, and there are now hundreds of affiliate churches all over the world.

Why don't more pastors teach prophecy? Perhaps some are afraid of getting it wrong or they want to avoid the frequent criticism that prophecies stir. Yet if we consider God's prophetic timeline and tune our hearts to the Holy Spirit, we will get it right enough for a remarkable number of souls to come into the kingdom of God.

Some believe prophecy is a negative message. They would rather teach and preach on how to live stress-free, walk in favor, and overcome anxiety. These types of sermons certainly can help. However, when 27 percent of the Bible is prophecy, we must not ignore it in our pulpits lest we fall short of preaching the whole counsel of God's Word (Acts 20:27).

Date Setters

Our generation has experienced a number of false alarms, people "crying wolf" and setting dates that come and go while their "prophecies" remain unfulfilled. Radio broadcaster and evangelist Harold Camping predicted the Rapture would occur on September 6, 1994. When September 6 passed, he revised the date to September 29 and later to October 2.[7] Years later Camping predicted that May 21, 2011, was the date the Rapture would occur.[8] When once again his prediction proved inaccurate, Camping reported that the Rapture and the end of the world would happen on October 21, 2011.[9] Yet October 21, 2011, came and went, and he was again proved wrong.

Another false alarm in our generation came from the writings of

Edgar Whisenant, a former NASA rocket engineer. He became well known for his booklet *88 Reasons Why the Rapture Could Be in 1988*. In his booklet Whisenant predicted that Jesus would return to rapture His church between September 11 and September 13, 1988.[10] Not surprisingly these dates came and went without incident. As a pastor during those years, I had a few members who purchased these booklets in bulk and distributed them to congregation members without my approval. This created a stir in our church that was not resolved until after the predictions failed.

These men were probably sincere in making their "calculations" and genuinely wanted to see people turn to Christ. But sincerity cannot replace God's Word. (See Matthew 24:36.)

Still another clamor burst on the Christian scene in January 1994 when John Hinkle, who was the pastor of Christ Church Los Angeles, predicted, "The most cataclysmic experience that the world has ever known since the Resurrection...is going to happen." Hinkle stated that God told him that on June 9, 1994, He would "rip the evil out of this world."[11] June 9, 1994, passed, and evil was still intact on our planet.

The truth is that we don't know the day or hour. Jesus said, "But concerning that day or hour no one knows, not even the angels in heaven, nor the Son, but only the Father" (Mark 13:32).

We don't know the day or hour, but we *do* know the times and seasons.

> Concerning the times and the seasons, brothers, you have no need that I write to you. For you know perfectly that the day of the Lord will come like a thief in the night. When they say, "Peace and safety!" then sudden destruction will come upon them as labor upon a woman with child, and they shall not escape.
>
> But you, brothers, are not in darkness so that this Day should overtake you as a thief.
>
> —1 Thessalonians 5:1–4

The good news is that prophecy belongs to God, not man. Erroneous prophecies are not His fault, and they don't make true, biblical prophecies any less true. Man did not invent the Bible or any of its prophecies, doesn't own them, and can't alter them: "For no prophecy at any time was produced by the will of man, but holy men moved by the Holy Spirit spoke from God" (2 Pet. 1:21).

We are responsible for diligently studying and being attentive to the true prophecies of God in the Bible. A superficial understanding of God's prophetic plan for the future leads to chaotic eschatology (that is, the study of the end times). If we start in the wrong place prophetically, we will end up in the wrong place prophetically. We start with the Bible, God's Word, and we interpret the conditions of the world based on Scripture. We do not interpret Scripture based on events in the contemporary world. Our starting point is what God said, not our imagination, news reports, or a scoffing culture.

Prophecy Brings Hope

Biblical prophecy is meant to bring hope and comfort for God's people while simultaneously delivering a warning to those not yet committed to Christ.

In *Hope in the Last Days* we are going to take a journey into understanding the astonishing events that are about to unfold. We will learn what will happen in the future before it appears in newspaper headlines. We will unravel the mysterious writings of the ancient biblical prophets by interpreting Scripture with Scripture. By gaining an understanding of these prophecies, you will never again fret over what may be about to transpire on the earth or fear the impending events foretold by God through His prophets. Instead, you will have surging hope in the midst of global difficulty. Why hope? Because hope rescues people from the trap of despair and gives them an expectation that God's promises will surely come true.

I know the value of hope. I served as pastor of Mount Hope Church in Lansing, Michigan, for more than thirty years. Hope is the precursor to genuine faith (Heb. 11:1). With hope we have vision, joy, and an inspiring and secure future. Without hope our hollow selves become filled with anxiety. Hopelessness is like hell on earth. A struggling couple feels hopeless when their efforts toward building a healthy relationship seem useless. A sense of hopelessness sets in when someone hears the doctor say their illness is terminal.

God never intended for us to walk in hopelessness. He intended for us to be people of faith, and faith is the substance of things we hope for. The biblical definition of *hope* is "confident expectation." From that hope springs the faith to do supernatural exploits. As a biblical prophet told us, "The people that do know their God shall be strong, and do exploits" (Dan. 11:32, KJV).

Hope is our enemy's main target. His goal is to destroy our vision and then steal our future. Hopelessness saps people's strength and makes them give up, believing there is no good future. Hopelessness is one of the most sinister traps we can fall into. The Bible pulls us out of that trap by giving us generous promises that compel us to look toward tomorrow with soaring hope and vibrant expectation.

God is calling us, as ambassadors of Christ, to be "hope distributors" in these last days. I have been encouraged lately by the quality of young leaders I see rising up. They have the marks of hope distributors. God is calling each of His ambassadors to give hope freely to those in our spheres of influence.

As believers we have every reason to hope.

In our study we will find that great news often comes right alongside dire warnings of impending trouble. For example, Jesus warned of increasing, frequent earthquakes in the last days (Matt. 24:7). That is not good news. On the other hand, other Bible prophecies tell of a coming spiritual outpouring in the last days. "'In the last days it shall be,' says God, 'that I will pour out My Spirit on all flesh; your sons and your daughters shall prophesy, your young men shall see visions, and your old men shall dream dreams'" (Acts 2:17).

Now that's great news! We will see good and bad happening simultaneously as the world is given a choice to turn toward God and His hope and protection or away from Him toward increasing darkness and confusion.

God is already fulfilling this positive prophecy. In Cuba, for instance, there were fewer than one hundred Assemblies of God churches in the 1990s. Today there are more than ten thousand Assemblies of God churches (including house churches) in communist Cuba.[12] God is divinely adding to His church.

The past couple of years have brought a flood of news articles about Christianity's growth, particularly in Muslim countries.[13] Some evangelists are now reporting that Muslims are turning to Jesus Christ at a "historic rate."[14] And in Egypt, revival is sweeping through at this moment.[15] Even in the midst of the most difficult circumstances, God is breaking through in a final roundup.

Indonesia, the largest Muslim nation in the world, had a very small Christian population just thirty years ago, but now two million Indonesian Muslims are turning to Christ each year.[16] The gospel of Jesus Christ seems even more powerful in countries with oppressive governments and persecution.

Where do you suppose the greatest growth of evangelical Christians is happening today? One place is Iran. That's right, Iran![17] Ancient Persia is experiencing unprecedented revival. In fact, six of the top ten countries experiencing the greatest revival are Muslim nations.[18] God has not abandoned these people but is keeping His promise to pour out His Spirit on all flesh (Joel 2:28–29; Acts 2:17–18).

It's exactly as Jesus prophesied: "I will build My church, and the gates of Hades shall not prevail against it" (Matt. 16:18).

Sealed Prophecies

As Jesus builds His church, He is unlocking secrets we will need to understand. After providing Daniel with a shocking prophetic overview of the last days, the angel Gabriel instructed him, "Go your way, Daniel. For these words are closed up and sealed until the time of the end" (Dan. 12:9; see also v. 4). The words "closed up" actually come from a Hebrew word meaning "encrypted" or "encoded." The word "sealed" means "preserved," like a sealed canning jar used to preserve food.

These things written in prophecy have been closed up and sealed for a future time—a time that is now coming upon us. God is swiftly unsealing and decoding these prophecies as we approach Christ's coming.

God meant for His people to understand the cryptic prophecies relating to the last days. For followers of Jesus Christ, there is no fear, only an exciting hope promised by Jesus Himself. He said, "When these things begin to happen, look up and lift up your heads, for your redemption is drawing near" (Luke 21:28), and "Let not your heart be troubled....I am going to prepare a place for you....I will come again and receive you to Myself, that where I am, you may be also" (John 14:1–3).

The apostle Paul wrote, "Now may the God of hope fill you with all joy and peace in believing, so that you may abound in hope, through the power of the Holy Spirit" (Rom. 15:13). And the apostle John shared the words of Jesus: "Because you have kept My word of patience, I also will keep you from the hour of temptation which shall come upon the entire world, to test those who dwell on the earth" (Rev. 3:10).

Jesus cried out, "Come to Me, all you who labor and are heavily burdened, and I will give you rest" (Matt. 11:28). In Revelation we read, "The Spirit and the bride say, 'Come'" (22:17).

I mentioned Hollywood earlier, and it seems Jesus is "speaking" through a number of films in the last decade or so to grab public attention, as if He is crying out, "Come to Me now!" These are just a few of the Christian titles the Holy Spirit has uniquely used to draw people to God:

+ *90 Minutes in Heaven*

+ *Facing the Giants*

+ *Fireproof*

- *God's Not Dead*
- *Heaven Is for Real*
- *Left Behind*
- *Miracles From Heaven*
- *War Room*
- *Woodlawn*

God, in His amazing love, is calling to this world and using every means available.

God Is a God of Order

When we understand God's ordered timeline for prophecy and adhere to the hermeneutical laws of eschatology, we will get the ancient biblical prophecies right. If we don't, we will get them wrong most of the time, caving in to human speculations.

In his book *Final Signs*, Ed Hindson offers insight on how some people approach the study of Bible prophecy. First, we begin with *biblical facts* as written in God's Word. The facts don't change. Second, we make *assumptions* based on the facts. For example, the doctrine of the Rapture is a fact based on 1 Thessalonians 4:16–18; 1 Corinthians 15:51–55; and John 14:3. Since God promised that believers are not appointed to His wrath (1 Thess. 5:9), we assume the Rapture will occur before God's wrath pours onto the earth during the Tribulation period. Third, we make *speculations*[19]—and this is where we get into trouble. Making calculated assumptions based on biblical facts is perfectly fine. Forming opinions and even making cautious speculations based on those assumptions is acceptable. But it is not OK to preach our personal speculations as absolute facts.

I will do my best to limit personal speculations in this book and to give you the facts just as the ancient prophets reported them to us, along with potential scenarios that may soon unfold. We are going to learn so much!

Prepare to gain a greater understanding of Bible prophecy, a deeper hope, and a more active faith than you have ever experienced in the past. Let's begin our journey into a bright and hopeful future!

Chapter 2

AVOIDING PROPHETIC PITFALLS AND DEFINING ESCHATOLOGICAL TERMS

[The Holy Spirit] will tell you things that are to come.
—JESUS, JOHN 16:13

I WAS TEACHING A message on Bible prophecy in Bad Axe, Michigan, explaining how close we are to the coming of the Lord, when something unusual happened. At the close of the message, I gave an invitation for people to come to Jesus. Many people dashed to the altar to receive Christ.

Then I gave one final appeal, asking, "Are you ready to meet God? Do you really believe in Jesus?" At that very moment, lightning struck near the building with a thunderous crash. All the windows lit up. Just then an older man sprinted from the back of the auditorium to the altar so he could pray the prayer of salvation. The man approached me after the service.

"Sir, I want to thank you for your presentation tonight," he whispered gently. "When you asked, 'Do you believe in Jesus?' and the thunder struck, I knew I had to make my peace with God tonight. That lightning was a great addition to your presentation. You ought to consider leaving it in your routine."

I laughed. Imagine if preachers could actually add lightning to their "routines." Maybe more people would dash to the altars!

Some Will Miss Their Hour of Visitation

Unfortunately many events in the end times will catch people by surprise just as the lightning caught that elderly man by surprise. But we shouldn't really be surprised by what is coming. Did you know there are more than eighteen hundred references to the second coming of Christ in the Old Testament? Seventeen Old Testament books give it great prominence. Yet many people never give it any thought.

Jesus Christ, at His first coming, fulfilled more than three hundred Old Testament prophecies concerning the Messiah.[1] The chances of any one person fulfilling just forty-eight Messianic prophecies is 1 in 10^{157} (10 with 157 zeros after it).[2] In other words, it is a mathematical impossibility that anyone other than Jesus Christ could be the Messiah. He met 100 percent of the prophetic criteria. Here are just a few of the familiar prophecies concerning His first coming:

+ He would be born of a virgin (Isa. 7:14).

+ He would be born in Bethlehem (Mic. 5:2).

+ He would become a sacrificial offering for sin and healing (Isa. 53).

+ He would be pierced (Zech. 12:10).

+ He would be "cut off" or executed (Dan. 9:24–26).

+ He would be resurrected (Ps. 16:8–10; 22:19–24).

Yet for every one prophecy concerning the first coming of Christ, there are eight that prophesy His return. How much more attention should we pay to His second coming! All the prophecies of His first coming were fulfilled literally, so we can expect all the prophecies of His second coming to be fulfilled literally as well.

If we don't expect literal fulfillment of prophecies, we invite massive problems. In spite of the hundreds of prophecies foretelling Christ's first coming, the vast majority of the Jewish scholars and religious leaders missed it! This carried a heavy price. They turned away during the most critical moment in human history—the moment of God's personal visitation on earth. Jesus spelled out the result:

When He came near, He beheld the city and wept over it, saying, "If you, even you, had known even today what things would bring you peace! But now they are hidden from your eyes. For the days will come upon you when your enemies will build an embankment around you and surround you, and press you in on every side. They will dash you, and your children within you, to the ground. They will not leave one stone upon another within you, because you did not know the time of your visitation."

—Luke 19:41–44

Because of their clumsy, pick-and-choose theology and failure to genuinely discern the ancient prophecies, religious leaders became disoriented, adrift, and careless. They inserted their own human ideas and traditions about the Messiah, nullifying the work of God's Word in their midst (Mark 7:13). They missed their moment.

Today some professing Christian leaders are in danger of missing their moment as well. They cherry-pick the Scriptures, taking what they like and ignoring the rest. Late apologist Dr. Walter Martin once warned that the greatest danger to churches today are men who wear the cross of Christ and stand behind pulpits but are unfaithful to the Word of God.[3] Amen!

In this chapter we will look at some of the most common mistakes, errors, and false beliefs surrounding biblical prophecy. First, let me present a brief overview of our terms.

Defining Prophetic Terms

+ **Prophecy**—a Holy Spirit–inspired foretelling or predicting of an event that is yet future, given through the biblical prophets (2 Pet. 1:21), not to be confused with simple prophetic words that come through sermons and other utterances (1 Cor. 14:1, 5).

+ **Theology**—the study of God, His character, and His nature.

+ **Replacement theology**—sometimes called "fulfillment theology" or "supersessionism," it holds that the Christian church has succeeded the Israelites as the chosen people of God, or that the new covenant has replaced or superseded the Mosaic and Davidic covenants. This theology says that because the Jews rejected Jesus as their Messiah, they are consequently condemned, forfeiting the promises of God's covenant with them.

+ **Eschatology**—the biblical study of end-time events.

+ **Hermeneutics**—the philosophy and methodology of biblical text interpretation; the study of the principles of interpretation of the Bible.

+ **Last days**—sometimes refers to the recent past. For example, in Hebrews 1:2, we read that God "has in these last days spoken to us by His Son." Obviously from the context, the writer is speaking about recently past days. But when *last days*, *latter days*, or *latter times* is used in prophetic writings, it refers to a time in which the return of Christ is rapidly approaching. For example, in Ezekiel 38 we read about the "latter days." This is a time when Israel is once again a nation. Obviously when Paul spoke of the last days in 2 Timothy 3:1, writing, "Know this: In the last days perilous times will come," he was referring to a future time, not the past.

  For the sake of this book, I define the *last days* as having begun on May 14, 1948, when Israel was reborn as a nation. This seems to be the indicator that the final countdown has begun.

+ **Hope**—from the Greek meaning "an expectation of good." It also means "a joyful and confident expectation of deliverance and eternal salvation."[4] Hope is the quality of belief that allows faith to operate effectively in receiving God's promises. Hope is our goal throughout this study.

+ **Rapture**—a future event when Christ will snatch true Christians from the earth. Those who have died in Christ will be raised and given glorified bodies, and those believers who are still alive will be caught up together with them in the clouds to meet the Lord in the air. (See 1 Corinthians 15:50–58; 1 Thessalonians 4:13–18.)

+ **Pretribulation Rapture**—the belief that Jesus will come for His bride (the church) prior to the Tribulation.

+ **Midtribulation Rapture**—the belief that Jesus will come for His bride (the church) in the middle of the Tribulation when the Antichrist moves his own image into the Jewish temple.

+ **Posttribulation Rapture**—the belief that Christians will go through the Great Tribulation without deliverance from heaven. Those who believe in a posttribulation Rapture see the Rapture as simultaneous with the appearing of Jesus Christ at His return to earth.

+ **Pre-wrath Rapture**—a twist on the midtribulation Rapture theory. This belief suggests that Jesus will remove His people prior to God's wrath being poured out on the world.

+ **Partial Rapture**—the belief that only those who are somehow sanctified enough will participate in the Rapture. It seems to be a comingling of salvation by works and grace. How people would know whether they are "sanctified enough" to be taken to heaven in the Rapture is unclear in this belief.

+ **Day of Christ**—a biblical reference either to the Rapture, which is distinctly different from the Second Coming, or to the period of God's judgment on the earth (1 Cor. 1:8; Phil. 1:6, 10; 2 Thess. 2:2).

+ **Day of the Lord**—a biblical reference to the Tribulation when the wrath of God envelops the earth (Joel 1:14–16; 2:1–3; Zeph. 1:13–15; 2:2; 1 Thess. 5:2; 2 Pet. 3:10).

+ **Tribulation**—the final seven years of human government. This period is known as Daniel's seventieth week, the missing piece in the seventy-week (490-year) prophecy of Daniel 9:24. Almost all biblical prophecies that remain unfulfilled relate to this period in human history when the world will unite under a world government led by the Antichrist. It will be the greatest hour of supreme agony in history (Matt. 24:21), will feature a more frightening holocaust than Adolf Hitler's, and will eventually give way to a cashless society where no transactions can be made without a personal mark of allegiance to the world leader, the Antichrist.

+ **Great Tribulation**—the last half of the Tribulation. The Tribulation period is clearly divided into two sections: the first forty-two months and the final forty-two months. The midpoint is when the Antichrist announces himself to be God. The final half of the Tribulation is called the Great Tribulation as twenty-one rapid-fire judgments slam the earth and things go from bad to worse. This period will end when Jesus Christ returns with His saints from heaven at Armageddon. (See Daniel 12:1; Matthew 24:21–22; Revelation 6–19.)

+ **Final** *shabua*—the term I often use for the final
  seven years of human government, also known as the
  Tribulation. The Hebrew word *shabua* means "week"
  or "seven."

+ **Antichrist**—the final human world leader during the
  final *shabua* (last seven years). He will be adored by
  the masses, empowered by Satan, and promoted by
  the global religious personality known as the False
  Prophet.

+ **Armageddon**—last gathering of earth's armies in the
  final moments before Christ's second coming (Zech.
  14:1–4, 12; Rev. 16:12–16; 19:11–21).

+ **Millennium**—derived from Latin, it simply means
  "one thousand years." In eschatology, it refers to the
  thousand-year earthly reign of Christ initiated immediately after the Antichrist forces are defeated at
  Armageddon (Rev. 20:1–6).

+ **Amillennialism**—the belief that there will be no literal thousand-year reign of Christ on earth, but that
  Revelation 20:1–6 and other scriptures are allegorical.

+ **Postmillennialism**—the belief that Jesus expects His
  church to disciple all nations before He can return.
  Those who hold this view believe that most people will
  be saved and gradually usher in a sort of golden age of
  peace and prosperity, after which Christ will return to
  earth to bring an eternal order.

+ **Premillennialism**—the belief that Jesus will literally and physically return to the earth before the
  Millennium.

+ **Second Coming**—the future return of Jesus Christ
to earth, not to be confused with the Rapture of the
church (Zech. 14:4; Rev. 19:11–21).

+ **First resurrection**—the raising of all believers, which
takes place in various phases. Those who died in
Christ will reunite with their earthly bodies and be
given glorified bodies, just like Jesus (1 Cor. 15:20;
Rev. 20:4–6). At the Rapture believers will experience
a stage of the first resurrection. Those who died for
Christ during the Tribulation period will rise when
Christ comes back at Armageddon, just before the
millennial kingdom begins (Rev. 20:4).

+ **Second resurrection**—those who participate in
the second resurrection, which takes place after the
thousand-year reign of Christ on earth, are the wicked
and unbelieving whose spirits abide now in Hades
(hell's prison). They will be judged at the Great White
Throne judgment and ultimately cast into the lake of
fire (Rev. 20:15).

+ **Judgment seat of Christ**—the judgment of believers
after the Rapture and before the Second Coming. It
does not involve salvation, for only the saved go before
the judgment seat of Christ to receive rewards for
their service in Christ while on the earth. There will
be no condemnation at this judgment (Rom. 14:9–12;
2 Cor. 5:8–10).

+ **Great white throne judgment**—occurs after the
millennial kingdom at the dreadful second resurrection, when the incarcerated spirits of those who never
accepted Christ in this life will be reunited with their
physical bodies, changed into bodies that can feel but
not die. Everyone who stands before God at this judgment will be declared guilty and assigned to *gehenna*

(hell) for eternity (Rev. 20:11–21:8), experiencing
eternal separation, darkness, and pain in the garbage
dump of all creation.

Don't worry about memorizing or fully understanding each term. Rather, check back here as needed. Each term will become clearer along the way.

Caution Against Sloppy Eschatology

Some Christians will miss the signs of the times because of complacency, but many more will miss them because of careless theology and sloppy eschatology—both based on weak or preconceived understandings of the Bible and God's plan. Only the Bible provides a solid foundation for theology and eschatology that won't fail us in perilous times.

And yet so many are losing their grip on biblical truth. In 2015 when the United States Supreme Court ruled in favor of same-sex marriage, some leaders once considered to be evangelical supported and even promoted this radical and perverse concept of marriage. When confronted, they often quip back with phrases like, "There are not that many scriptures on the subject," or "Jesus never spoke about it, so it's not a big issue." Some ignored almost everything in the Bible except the words of Jesus, forgetting that Jesus Himself defined *marriage* (Matt. 19:5).

Some pastors similarly make light of end-time prophecies. I have heard some say, "You cannot be sure about anything, including biblical doctrines such as prophecy," and "Scripture is fluid and adaptable to the culture."

While some of these pastors enjoy almost celebrity-like acceptance by the secular news media, they are sliding into deeper apostasy from which they may never return. Culture tries to dictate what is and is not acceptable doctrine. As a result some believers have defected from the faith by worshipping the creature's opinions over the Creator's

Word. No wonder Jesus asked, "When the Son of Man comes, will He find faith on the earth?" (Luke 18:8).

Like the Jewish leaders of Jesus's earthly time, these pastors flounder in their understanding of prophecy. Our eschatology cannot be based on human opinions, personal revelations, cultural preferences, or human imagination. The foundation must always be Scripture, enlightened by the Holy Spirit to our hearts and minds.

Let's look into what causes tangled-up theology and disheveled eschatology.

A shallow understanding of the Bible and God's plan

The Bible is not a man-made book, although God used men as partners in writing it. Rather, "know this first of all, that no prophecy of the Scripture is a matter of one's own interpretation. For no prophecy at any time was produced by the will of man, but holy men moved by the Holy Spirit spoke from God" (2 Pet. 1:20–21). Accordingly, "study to show yourself approved by God, a workman who need not be ashamed, rightly dividing the word of truth" (2 Tim. 2:15).

I remember a retired army sergeant in our church who was a soul winner and valued member. But then something happened. His demeanor changed. Some financial expert had convinced him that Christians will go through the Great Tribulation. I noticed that this man's soul-winning efforts ceased. His joy disappeared. His attendance at church became sporadic, and his giving declined. When I talked with him, I felt an unusual anxiety emanating from him. He tried to pressure me to prepare the congregation for the Great Tribulation. He had purchased land in northern Michigan where he was building an underground hideout and a bomb shelter and storing weapons and food caches in order to survive the approaching wrath of God. When I gently reminded him of Christ's promises of peace, he left the church and never came back. I never saw him again.

If he had dug into God's Word for himself, he would have found peace instead of anxiety:

Peace I leave with you. My peace I give to you. Not as the world gives do I give to you. Let not your heart be troubled, neither let it be afraid.

—JOHN 14:27

I have told you these things so that in Me you may have peace. In the world you will have tribulation. But be of good cheer. I have overcome the world.

—JOHN 16:33

A shallow understanding of the Bible will take us off track.

Twisted thinking

The word *twisted* is exactly the same as the word *wicked* in the Bible. In fact, the terms can almost always be interchanged without altering the meaning of the text. A candlewick is twisted thread, a wicker basket is twisted bamboo, and twisted thinking is wicked thinking. As Peter wrote, "Keep in mind that the patience of our Lord means salvation, even as our beloved brother Paul has also written to you according to the wisdom given to him. As in all his letters, he writes about these things, in which some things are hard to understand, which the unlearned and unstable distort, as they also do the other Scriptures, to their own destruction" (2 Pet. 3:15–16).

Today there are all types of twisted thinking about the Bible. Most attack its veracity or integrity. Many denominations no longer take the Bible literally. Rather, they allegorize the literal truths of the Bible. For instance, I was raised in a church that espoused the amillennial view. I was taught that everything in prophecy was symbolic, that the Book of Revelation was merely an allegory of the struggle between good and evil. "You can't understand it anyway, so don't even try. It will only confuse you," my pastor told us during our catechism class.

Yet we are told in Revelation 1:3 that we will be blessed if we read this book, hear it, and keep it (that is, remember it). Whenever you allegorize God's Word, you open up the possibility of innumerable different interpretations, none grounded in Scripture. Nobody could possibly keep up with all the latest interpretations if we leaned on human brilliance instead of God's Word. Yet when we stop taking the Bible as literal, we elevate human thinking over God's thinking. Our thinking rapidly becomes twisted without the straightening effect of God's eternal truth on us.

Viewing a "new" revelation or prophecy as equal with Scripture

Many years ago as a young pastor I attended a meeting where a self-proclaimed bishop told of his visit to heaven. He declared that God showed him, "Those who believe in the Rapture are deceived." He went on to give an allegorical and peculiar explanation of the apocalypse, which he claimed came directly from the lips of Jesus during his visit to heaven.[5]

When the majority of the attendees started shaking their heads, dismissing his visions, the bishop became visibly disturbed and forcefully asserted, "My experience was just as valid as St. John's revelation."[6] I shuddered at his words because he put himself and his strange allegorical "revelations" on the same level as the apostle John's writing in the Scriptures.

Although this man was a pleasant and likable person, he was propagating a very unscriptural "revelation." The apostle John cautioned us to test the spirits to see if they are of God: "Beloved, do not believe every spirit, but test the spirits to see whether they are from God, because many false prophets have gone out into the world" (1 John 4:1).

I believe there are real, Christ-loving, Jesus-exalting prophets in the church today who bring significant words of encouragement and warning to the body of Christ. On the other hand, there are self-appointed prophets who have little concept of true, biblical prophecy.

For example, I heard a preacher once say, "Whenever you read the term *last days* in the Bible, it is referring only to the last days of the old covenant." He then went on to describe the second coming of Christ as allegorical rather than literal.[7] I'm sure he was sincere, but the question is this: if Jesus came literally the first time and promised to come again, why would His first coming be literal and His second coming be allegorical?

Beware of those who substitute their own views for the Bible's clear teaching and label it "prophecy."

A Few Sensible Rules for Understanding Prophecy

Unless a Scripture text clearly indicates that it is symbolic or figurative, it should be taken literally.

Author Dr. Ron Rhodes has a reliable saying: "When plain sense makes good sense, seek no other sense, lest you end up in nonsense."[8] Start with the plain sense and go no further if the meaning seems clear. Otherwise you will end up interpreting everything in the Bible according to your own imagination and perspective.

When you encounter a symbol or allegory in the Bible, you will find clues to its meaning elsewhere in Scripture. Let Scripture interpret Scripture. Even in the Book of Revelation the symbols are many times explained later in John's writings. For example, a person could ask, "What are the golden candlesticks John writes about in Revelation?" All you have to do is read a little further to find out that he is talking about the churches. When we get crafty by assigning arbitrary meanings, we behave as those Peter wrote about: "Some things are hard to understand, which the unlearned and unstable distort, as they also do the other Scriptures, to their own destruction" (2 Pet. 3:16).

When you take literal language and turn it into figurative speech, you are at the mercy of whoever decides what it means. When we take the Bible literally, we don't ignore that the Bible contains both allegory and figurative speech, but we affirm that figurative speech in the Bible is always meant to illustrate an important spiritual truth or principle, and we will always know when it is an allegory or a parable.

Jesus consistently interpreted the Old Testament literally and affirmed its divine inspiration. If the literal interpretation of Scripture is good enough for Jesus, it is good enough for us when studying end-times prophecy and everything else in His precious Word.

Pay attention to context.

Is the text speaking to Israel or the Jewish people? Is it speaking to a certain nation or leader? Is it speaking to Christians? Who is the audience? God typically deals with three different groups in prophecy: Israel, the church, and unbelievers.

The Old Testament was written originally by, to, and for Jews. The words and idioms were intelligible to them, just as Jesus's words were when He lived on the earth. We should have some awareness of the life and times in which Scripture was written. Spiritual principles will be timeless but often can't be properly appreciated without some knowledge of the background.

In addition, context matters. As you read, ask, "What is the context of this passage?" Isolated verses can be used to mean anything, as we have seen demonstrated by a hodgepodge of faulty modern prophets. Instead, ask, "What does Scripture say before the verse? What does Scripture say after the verse?"

As it has been wisely stated, "The interpretation of a specific verse must not contradict the total teaching of Scripture on a point. Individual verses do not exist as isolated fragments, but as parts of a whole." [9] And remember: Jesus Christ fulfilled literally all the prophecies concerning His first coming. So He will fulfill literally all the prophecies concerning His second coming.

Most importantly remember the purpose of prophecy.

"Worship God! For the testimony of Jesus is the spirit of prophecy" (Rev. 19:10). Cultic and twisted interpretations of Scripture present another Jesus and another gospel, leading to error and ensuing judgment (2 Cor. 11:3–4; Gal. 1:6–9; Rev. 20:11–15). The point of prophecy is that we would worship God and understand the testimony of Christ!

Further suggestions

When reading biblical prophecy, here are a few more foundational guidelines that will help you gain a clearer understanding.

As you read, ask, "What does the word mean?" This may require some research that goes beyond looking up the word in a dictionary. You may want to obtain a copy of *Vine's Expository Dictionary of New Testament Words* or a good Greek and Hebrew lexicon, or find one of these resources online.

As you read, pray, "Father, I ask that Your Spirit will enlighten and guide me in my study." (See John 16:12–15, 1 Corinthians 2:9–11.) The Holy Spirit is the Spirit of truth who guides us into all truth (John 16:13). We can only understand God's Word by His enlightenment through the Holy Spirit (Eph. 4:18). The Holy Spirit will guide you into all truth in a way that is consistent with His nature, His Word, and His purposes.

You *Can* Understand Bible Prophecy!

Keeping these simple things in mind, we can be confident that common, ordinary Christians can understand Bible prophecy without relying on capricious contemporary explanations. Jesus taught with clarity, with the full expectation that His followers would understand His meaning. Scripture alone, enlightened by the Holy Spirit, makes us capable and proficient in understanding.

Chapter 3

THE SPIRIT OF PROPHECY

HOW I PERSONALLY MET JESUS IN BIBLE PROPHECY

For the testimony of Jesus is the spirit of prophecy.
—REVELATION 19:10

IMAGINE A MAN who foretold the future so accurately that all his critics could do was try to insist that his book must have been written after the fact! This is not some Nostradamus or a secular seer or necromancer—this man's prophetic forecasts are found in the Holy Bible itself. His name is Daniel.

Daniel is remembered mostly for surviving the lions' den. But Daniel's book contains the Bible's most astonishing, accurate prophecies regarding world events. That is why critics and skeptics allege that Daniel's book was written after these world events unfolded. The prophecies are so meticulous and accurate that they threaten their critics' humanistic foundation of knowledge.

For example, Daniel received revelation about Alexander the Great, the four generals who followed him, and the maniac Antiochus IV Epiphanes, who rose up in the latter years of the Grecian Empire. Daniel's prophecies told exact details of what would happen three hundred years later!

Here's the interesting thing: many of Daniel's prophecies are yet to happen; they concern a time in the future. For that reason, the Book of Daniel is one of the most important books in the Bible to help us understand coming world events.

Interestingly my personal story intersects with the Book of Daniel and shows how such prophetic books can speak truth to the heart of man—even when that heart is sinful, as mine was.

How I Met Jesus in Daniel 2

In 1971 I was serving in the US Navy aboard the USS *Reasoner* (DE-1063). I had been raised in a relatively lifeless denominational church. I was quite fond of my sinful lifestyle and didn't want to trade it for some sad, gloomy life in church. I stayed away from people who called themselves "saved." They were just too judgmental and weird for me.

One day, however, while working aboard the ship, I noticed two sailors holding up their index fingers and smiling every time they saw each other. I noticed that each time one saw the other, they raised those index fingers again. Their names were Howard Malone and Terry Miller. Finally, one day I asked Howard, "Why do you hold up your index finger every time you see Terry?"

"Don't you know?" Howard responded. "That means there's only one way to God—and it's Jesus!"

"Oh, ah, OK," I said, walking away so I wouldn't get roped into a religious conversation. But I couldn't help noticing there was something different about those two sailors. They were always smiling, upbeat, and joyful. I couldn't get them out of my mind. Later I would learn that Howard was right. There *is* only one way to God, and that is through Jesus Christ.

> I am the way, the truth, and the life. No one comes to the Father except through Me.
> —John 14:6

> There is one God and one mediator between God and men, the Man Christ Jesus.
> —1 Timothy 2:5

But none of that made sense to me then. I had as a young man attended catechism. I believed the right things. I knew the Apostles' Creed, the Lord's Prayer, Psalm 23, and John 3:16 by heart. I believed in God the Father Almighty, the Creator of heaven and earth. I believed in His only begotten Son, Jesus Christ, who was conceived of the Holy Spirit and born of the blessed virgin. I believed He lived a sinless life, went about doing good and healing people who were oppressed of the devil. I believed that Jesus died on the cross, not for His sin, but for the sin of the world. I believed He rose from the dead, ascended into heaven, and promised to come back again to judge the living and the dead.[1]

That was my orthodoxy. *Orthodoxy* simply means "correct doctrine." The problem was I had no orthopraxy, which means "correct behavior" or "correct experience." It's possible to hold correct beliefs without being born again. That was my condition. I was orthodox in my beliefs but was not a practicing Christian. Far from it. In fact, my life was spiritually empty and out of control. If I had died then, I would have gone directly to the place of the damned (Hades, or hell) to await the terrible great white throne judgment. Thank God for the radar room on that ship.

Sneaking Up to the Radar Room

I was drawn to Howard and Terry's joy. They were not like other Christians I had met who seemed harsh and extreme. Howard and Terry liked me even though I didn't share their lifestyle. So I began sneaking up to the radar room at night (after a few drinks) to talk with Terry about the Bible. Terry was like no Christian I had ever met in my life. He seemed to really know Jesus and to love me and care about my future. He always told me about the great church he and Howard were attending. It sounded like no other church I had seen.

One Sunday I told Terry that if he ever needed a ride to church, I would be happy to take him and his friends. To my surprise, on Monday afternoon Terry approached me and said, "Dave, we need a ride to church tonight."

I reminded him that this was Monday, not Sunday, but he assured me there was a church service on Monday night. "After all," he replied with a smile, "you promised."

Terry and three other guys loaded into my canary-yellow Ford Futura, with a big hood scoop, four on the floor, stainless steel exhaust, and really bad shocks. We started from San Diego and went bouncing north on Interstate 5. The guys in the car were singing "Amazing Grace," and it sounded so beautiful. Of course, that was at the time when Judy Collins's rendition of "Amazing Grace" was popular in bars and nightclubs.

We drove for miles and miles. I finally asked Terry, "How far is this church?"

"Only about 75 miles north of here," he replied nonchalantly. So we drove some more. Finally, we arrived at the corner of Sunflower and Fairview in Costa Mesa. A big tent was set up because the congregation had outgrown their small church. What I saw there was completely new to me: hippies, businesspeople, young people, older people, and what seemed like thousands heading into the tent. It was a Bible study night, and the huge tent was packed to capacity.

That night I heard things I had never heard before. People were telling each other, "Praise the Lord," "Hallelujah," "God bless you, brother," and "Maranatha!" At first I wondered what kind of a cult Howard and Terry were recruiting me for, but then I saw something in the front row—a couple of sweet-looking, smiling nuns, wearing their habits. That comforted me. As we started to sing, the little nuns lifted their hands along with others in the tent. There was no pipe organ, just plenty of guitars, flutes, and the kind of music I appreciated as a twenty-year-old sailor.

Before long, the pastor, Chuck Smith, came up to his stool on the platform and began to teach verse by verse from Daniel 2. I was riveted.

Daniel's Background

Daniel had been taken captive by King Nebuchadnezzar of Babylon when he was still a teenager. This young Hebrew boy was filled with God's wisdom and was chosen to be one of the king's counselors, which turned out to be a very good choice. Young Daniel soon became the most valuable man in Nebuchadnezzar's kingdom.

King Nebuchadnezzar had conquered Jerusalem and carried away most of the Jewish people, putting them into captivity for seventy years. He rebuilt Babylon, turning it into a colossal city with a complex of impressive buildings, a palace, and hanging gardens with terraces and arches fully tended by professional gardeners. There was no place like it on earth.

One night Nebuchadnezzar had a troubling dream. He knew it was important, but he did not know the interpretation and apparently couldn't remember the finer details. So he consulted occultists, astrologers, and magicians and commanded them to reveal what he had dreamed and give him the interpretation. The magicians and sorcerers were helpless. They could neither tell the dream nor interpret it, making the king furious (Dan. 2:1–13).

A Prophecy for Then and Now

In his fury Nebuchadnezzar ordered all the counselors to be executed. When Daniel heard about this, he quickly approached the captain of the king's guard and informed him that God would reveal the king's dream and interpretation. Daniel mustered his prayer partners, and they prayed as if their lives depended on it—because they did (Dan. 2:14–18).

The prayers paid off, and God revealed the prophetic dream and what it meant (Dan. 2:19–23). The dream foretold what would happen in the latter days—the time in which we now live: "There is a God in heaven who reveals secrets and makes known to King Nebuchadnezzar *what shall be in the latter days*" (Dan. 2:28, emphasis added). This was not just a dream for their time but for ours as well.

With amazing courage Daniel explained the dream and the interpretation to the king.

You, O king, were watching, and there was a great image. This great image, whose brightness was excellent, stood before you. And its form was awesome. This image's head was of fine gold, its breast and its arms of silver, its belly and its thighs of bronze, its legs of iron, its feet partly of iron and partly of clay. You watched until a stone was cut out without hands which struck the image upon its feet, which were of iron and clay, and broke them to pieces. Then the iron, the clay, the bronze, the silver, and the gold were broken to pieces together, and became like the chaff of the summer threshing floors. And the wind carried them away so that not a trace of them was found. But the stone that struck the image became a great mountain and filled the whole earth.

—Daniel 2:31–35

Nebuchadnezzar's dream was of an image of a man with a head of gold, breast and arms of silver, midsection and thighs of brass or bronze, legs of iron, and feet partly of iron and partly of clay. The dream was simple, yet its prophetic significance is profound. Having set the table, Daniel continued, "This was the dream. Now we will tell its interpretation before the king" (Dan. 2:36).

Babylon

Daniel described the head of gold as representing Nebuchadnezzar himself and his Babylonian empire. His kingdom was given to him by God and filled with strength, power, and glory. Nebuchadnezzar must have been happy to hear this.

You, O king, are the king of [earthly] kings, to whom the God of heaven has given the kingdom, the power, the strength and the glory; and wherever the sons of men dwell, and the beasts of the field, and the birds of the heavens, He has given them into your hand and has made you ruler over them all. You [king of Babylon] are the head of gold.

—Daniel 2:37–38, amp

Medo-Persia and Greece

Daniel continued, saying that the breast and arms of the image represented the empire that would rise up next in place of Babylon. The arms and chest represented the Mede and Persian leaders who would overthrow Babylon in the future. Daniel, perhaps understanding the king's ego, assured him that the next empire would be less powerful. The kingdom following that one, represented by the belly and thighs of brass, turned out to be the Grecian Empire.

> After you will arise another kingdom (Medo-Persia) inferior to you, and then a third kingdom of bronze (Greece under Alexander the Great), which will rule over all the earth.
> —DANIEL 2:39, AMP

Rome

After Greece another kingdom would arise, represented by the legs of iron. This was the empire that ruled when Jesus walked the earth, the Roman Empire. This picture of two legs offered a view of the two divisions of the Roman Empire, western and eastern. It is interesting to note that the western part of the Roman Empire, once Christian, is now primarily secular, but the eastern part of the old Roman Empire, which outlasted the western part, is mostly Muslim.

> Then a fourth kingdom (Rome) will be strong as iron, for iron breaks to pieces and shatters all things; and like iron which crushes things in pieces, it will break and crush all these [others].
> —DANIEL 2:40, AMP

A final human empire grows from the fourth

Daniel was shown the final world power when he spoke about the feet of the image, partly iron and partly clay, which evidently explained a revival of the Roman Empire in the last days. The ten toes most likely represent ten regions that were once a part of the old Roman Empire. This is the only part of the image that includes the same metal (iron) as the legs, representing the fourth kingdom, Rome.

Because this is depicted as a mixture of clay and iron, it will likely prove to be a fragile conglomeration of European nations or regions that form a world power in the last days. Later we will see how the final human world leader will make his appearance from this conglomerate kingdom.

> And as you saw the feet and toes, partly of potter's clay and partly of iron, it will be a divided kingdom; but there will be in it some of the durability *and* strength of iron, just as you saw the iron mixed with common clay. As the [ten] toes of the feet were partly of iron and partly of clay, so some of the kingdom will be strong, and *another* part of it will be brittle. And as you saw the iron mixed with common clay, so they will combine with one another in the seed of men; but they will not merge [for such diverse things or ideologies cannot unite], even as iron does not mix with clay.
>
> —Daniel 2:41–43, amp

Nebuchadnezzar's Dream

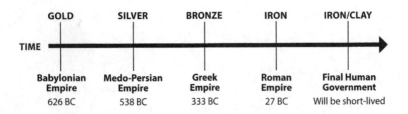

GOLD	SILVER	BRONZE	IRON	IRON/CLAY
Babylonian Empire	Medo-Persian Empire	Greek Empire	Roman Empire	Final Human Government
626 BC	538 BC	333 BC	27 BC	Will be short-lived

Note that the Roman Empire is the only world power that was not overthrown. It simply died out little by little.

Then Daniel described the millennial kingdom, the one we pray for when we say, "Thy kingdom come."

> In the days of those [final ten] kings the God of heaven will set up a kingdom that will never be destroyed, nor will its sovereignty be left for another people; but it will crush and put an end to all these kingdoms, and it will stand forever.

> Just as you saw that a stone was cut out of the mountain without hands and that it crushed the iron, the bronze, the clay, the silver and the gold, the great God has revealed to the king what will take place in the future; so the dream is true and its interpretation is trustworthy.
>
> —DANIEL 2:44–45, AMP

Now Daniel told what God revealed to him about this final human kingdom and how it will be short-lived. He saw how the stone not cut with human hands will grow to fill the entire earth, leaving all previous empires as a memory. This, of course, represents the coming of Christ to set up His earthly kingdom, when human governments are struck down for good.

History so far confirms the stunning accuracy of Daniel's interpretation. The Babylonian Empire lasted from 626 BC to 538 BC, when Babylon was conquered by Cyrus, king of Persia. The Medo-Persian Empire then lasted until Alexander the Great defeated the Persian armies at the Battle of Issus, marking the beginning of the Grecian Empire. Greece was defeated by the Romans in 146 BC, although the Roman Empire did not officially begin until Augustus became the first emperor in 27 BC.

The only part yet to be fulfilled before Christ returns to earth is the ten-region federation—the final world empire made up of partly strong and partly weak member nations. This will be the final world power and will last only a short time before Jesus Christ returns to earth to establish His physical kingdom.

Prophecy Brought Me to Jesus

I sat there in that tent listening as the teaching went on for over an hour. Pastor Chuck explained it all in a way I could understand. When he got to the part about a stone not cut with human hands (Dan. 2:34; 1 Pet. 2:7) that would grow to fill the entire earth, he explained that the stone represented Jesus Christ and His kingdom. Pastor Chuck then gave us all an opportunity to become a part of that kingdom. I raised my hand as fast as lightning. When I did, you would have thought I had caught a football. People started tackling me, and I heard, "Praise the Lord, brother," "God bless you," and "Hallelujah."

I prayed the prayer of salvation that night, asking Jesus to be my Lord and Savior. I was born again, and I have never been the same since. That is how I met Jesus in the prophetic teaching of Daniel chapter 2. The night I gave those guys a ride to church changed my life forever.

Perhaps you are like I was. You believe the right things but have never been born again. If that's the case, you can change it all now. Please see the appendix to learn how to ask Jesus to be your Savior and become a part of His kingdom.

Chapter 4

THE PROPHETIC CHRONOLOGY

NOTHING MAKES SENSE WITHOUT THIS

For God is not the author of confusion.
—1 CORINTHIANS 14:33

M Y WIFE AND I often walk out to St. Pete Beach, Florida, to the old Pass-a-Grille section, to watch the sun set over the Gulf of Mexico. It's beautiful, and the sun seems to kiss the sea before disappearing over the horizon. Each night someone gets the privilege of ringing the sunset bell on the beach, alerting residents of the small peninsula that the sun has set for the day. We never have to wonder when the sun will set. It's predictable thanks to the order God built into creation.

God's love of order pervades His creation. The earth rotates in perfect time. Billions of heavenly bodies in the universe all operate perfectly in their orbits and solar systems. From the splendor of space to the awe-inspiring details of the smallest of creatures, we see God's love for harmony and order.

Prophetic Order

Bible prophecy follows a designed order too. When we get the order right, it all makes sense. When we get the order wrong or have no idea of the timeline of prophetic events, we are left with confusion. Wherever God is ignored or left out, the consequences are chaos and confusion. This goes for biblical interpretation as well. Let's look at one of the most important biblical prophecies that sheds light on the prophetic timeline and helps us see how events will unfold.

Daniel 9 is one of the most noteworthy and amazing chapters in the whole Bible as it relates to the prophetic timeline. The year its events were occurring was 538 BC, and during this time Israel was toiling under the heavy hand of Babylon. Daniel was studying scriptures to gain insight into God's prophetic timeline. He wanted to know how much longer Israel would be under Babylonian rule. He found the answer in the prophetic writings of Jeremiah.

> This whole land shall be a desolation and an astonishment, and these nations will serve the king of Babylon seventy years.
>
> It shall come to pass when seventy years are finished that I will punish the king of Babylon and that nation, says the LORD, for their iniquity, and the land of the Chaldeans, and will make it perpetual desolations.
>
> —JEREMIAH 25:11–12

Daniel made some calculations based on Jeremiah's prophecy and realized that the end of the seventy years had almost arrived; in just a few more years, Israel's captivity would be over. Daniel believed Jeremiah and began to fast and pray with confession and humility. He understood that the reason Israel came into captivity was because his people had turned their backs on God's ways.

As a side note, let's recognize the parallels between Israel then and the United States now, because that is our immediate cultural context, and we are experiencing some of the same things in our own country. Evangelist Billy Graham said in his later years, "Our society strives to avoid any possibility of offending anyone—except God. Yet the farther we get from God, the more the world spirals out of control. My heart aches for America and its deceived people."[1]

Who could have imagined we would see the day when the White House was lit up with homosexual colors to celebrate same-sex marriage? Yet it happened on June 26, 2015, after the Supreme Court's decision to legally establish same-sex marriage. President Obama said it "was a moment worth savoring."[2]

Who would have thought we would see the day when the Empire State Building would carry the demon goddess Kali projected on thirty-three stories of its exterior? This happened on August 1, 2015, when the south side of the famous building was lit up with projected images of Kali, the Hindu goddess of death and destruction.[3]

Who could have predicted that undercover videos would leave people wondering whether the nation's largest abortion provider had ever, or would ever, attempt to sell human body parts?[4] Who would have thought that a bakery would be sued and forced out of business for not baking a gay couple a wedding cake?[5] Who ever would have guessed that a Christian county clerk would be thrown into jail for not issuing marriage licenses to same-sex couples?[6] Yet that's what happened.

Israel was in much the same condition as America is now when the Babylonians invaded, took control, and led the citizens into captivity that would last seventy years. Daniel, in his prayers, confessed the sins of his nation (Israel) as well as his own sins. Daniel was intimate with God, and the more intimate we are with God, the more we realize our imperfections and offenses toward God. The farther we are from God, the more callous our hearts are toward our own sin.

The Seventy Weeks and the Missing Seven Years

After Daniel's prayer, the ninth chapter then spells out God's timeline of human history. Respected nineteenth-century prophecy scholar Sir Edward Denny referred to Daniel's vision of the seventy weeks as "the backbone of prophecy."[7] He was exactly right. The vision begins, "While I was speaking and praying and confessing my sin and the sin of my people Israel, and presenting my supplication before the LORD my God…Gabriel, whom I had seen in the vision at the beginning…touched me about the time of the evening oblation" (Dan. 9:20–21). Gabriel then tells Daniel:

Seventy weeks have been determined for your people and upon your holy city, to finish the transgression, and to make an end of sins, and to make atonement for iniquity, and to bring in everlasting righteousness, and to seal up the vision and prophecy, and to anoint the Most Holy Place.

Know therefore and understand that from the going forth of the command to restore and to rebuild Jerusalem until the Prince Messiah shall be seven weeks, and sixty-two weeks. It shall be built again, with plaza and moat, even in times of trouble. After the sixty-two weeks Messiah shall be cut off and shall have nothing. And the troops of the prince who shall come shall destroy the city and the sanctuary. The end of it shall come with a flood. And until the end of the war desolations are determined. And he shall make a firm covenant with many for one week. But in the middle of the week he shall cause the sacrifice and the offering to cease. And on the wing of abominations shall come one who makes desolate, until the decreed destruction is poured out on the desolator.

—DANIEL 9:24–27

As Daniel prayed, the archangel Gabriel appeared to him. Gabriel offered comfort to Daniel's troubled heart and brought him fresh revelation. A *revelation* is a disclosure, an impartation that brings something hidden to light.

Here's how the revelation began: "Seventy weeks have been determined for your people and upon your holy city" (Dan. 9:24). Daniel wrote down what Gabriel said to him. In the Hebrew language, the word *week* is *shabua*, meaning "seven." These seventy sevens, or weeks, "have been determined for your people and upon your holy city." How do we know specifically that the weeks are speaking of years? We know because the Messiah, Jesus Christ, came in the precise number of years predicted by Gabriel: "Know therefore and understand that from the going forth of the command to restore and to rebuild

Jerusalem until the Prince Messiah shall be seven weeks, and sixty-two weeks" (Dan. 9:25).

Seven weeks of years equals 49 years. Sixty-two weeks of years equals 434 years. The total of the two added together is 483 years. That means that from the time the command would go forth in the future, there would be 483 years until the Jewish Messiah would be revealed.

This is precisely what happened. Artaxerxes, the Persian leader, gave the command to rebuild Jerusalem, and it took 49 years to complete (the first seven weeks; see the books of Nehemiah and Ezra). After 434 more years Jesus rode into Jerusalem on a young donkey. Based on this prophecy alone, nobody else could possibly be the Jewish Messiah. If the Jewish leaders had studied the prophecies of Daniel instead of their hand-me-down traditions, they would have known that Jesus was their Messiah: "None of the rulers of this age knew it. For had they known it, they would not have crucified the Lord of glory" (1 Cor. 2:8).

Gabriel then told about Christ's crucifixion: "After the sixty-two weeks Messiah shall be cut off and shall have nothing" (Dan. 9:26). To the religious leaders, Jesus seemed to "have nothing," meaning it appeared He accomplished nothing. He was cut off, executed. In their view He failed His mission. Yet that is precisely when the world began its transition into a mystery parenthetical age to await the restarting of Israel's prophetic clock, which would later initiate the remaining seven years.

Gabriel told Daniel that 490 years had been determined for the Jewish people and the city of Jerusalem. But there were only 483 years until Jesus the Messiah came. This leaves a missing seven-year period. What's going on here?

God inserted a time period before the completion of the seventy weeks, a parenthetical age that the Bible calls "a mystery."

> Now to Him who has power to establish you according to
> my gospel and the preaching of Jesus Christ, according to

the revelation of the mystery, which was kept secret for long
ages past.

—Romans 16:25

This parenthetical age was a mystery to the Old Testament
prophets. The word *mystery* in the Greek language is *mysterion*,
meaning "a hidden truth, a secret about God's plan, not because it
cannot be known today, but because it was kept secret by God in past
ages." [8] At just the right time, God revealed it through the apostles at
the beginning of the parenthetical church age. God kept these wonderful truths secret until the mystery age of grace began.

Timeline (not to scale)

When the Jewish leaders rejected their Messiah, having Him executed outside the northern gate of Jerusalem at the executioners' hill
called Golgotha, the prophetic clock stopped and a transition into the
parenthetical phase began. The transition was completed on the Day
of Pentecost. Enter the mystery parenthetical phase, known as the
church age, the age of grace, or the mystery age.

Although God is not finished with the nation of Israel or the
Jewish people, the prophetic clock paused in relation to His direct
and decisive dealings with the nation of Israel. When Jesus died, rose
from the dead, ascended back to heaven, and sent the Holy Spirit to
live within believers, the transition was made to this parenthetical

age. During this time, God's prophetic clock for Israel would remain silent—until the signing of a seven-year peace agreement and its ultimate confirmation by the Antichrist, the rising world leader.

The Prince Who Shall Come

Next Gabriel introduces Daniel (and us) to a personality he called "the prince who shall come."

> And the troops of the prince who shall come shall destroy
> the city and the sanctuary.
> —DANIEL 9:26

The troops that destroyed Jerusalem and the temple in AD 70 were Romans. The Antichrist "prince" will come from the same people. The destruction and decimation of AD 70 was but a preview of a coming main event.

Gabriel continued:

> The end of it shall come with a flood. And until the end of
> the war desolations are determined. And he shall make a
> firm covenant with many for one week. But in the middle
> of the week he shall cause the sacrifice and the offering to
> cease. And on the wing of abominations shall come one who
> makes desolate, until the decreed destruction is poured out
> on the desolator.
> —DANIEL 9:26–27

Gabriel forecasted constant trouble, wars, and conflicts for the people of Israel "until the end of the war desolations are determined" (v. 26).

Today Israel is surrounded by enemies and is becoming more isolated from world powers and ally nations. Israel is not initiating threats against its Islamic neighbors, but the same cannot be said of those other nations with regard to Israel. Because of the threats, Israel will be willing to reach out for a peace agreement.

You may have observed that the tide of anti-Semitism is rising again. Islamic immigrants are flooding into the European Union, and many European Jews are wondering if it is time to leave.[9] Anti-Semitic crimes have been doubling almost annually, including assault, harassment, arson, and property damage. Across London anti-Semitic crimes rose by 138 percent between 2013/14 and 2014/15.[10] Dr. Jack Van Impe called anti-Semitism "a cancer that never seems to heal."[11]

Eventually the Antichrist will cut a peace deal with Israel and other nations (Dan. 9:26–27). But as a master truce breaker, he will violate the agreement exactly forty-two months later, claim to be God incarnate, and move his own image into the new temple in Jerusalem, where he will set up his new headquarters. Antiochus IV Epiphanes was a type of the coming end-time leader, but he was not the complete fulfillment of this prophecy. We know this is a future event because Jesus warned His followers about this as being yet to come (Matt. 24:15–31). The apostle Paul also told us it is yet a future event (2 Thess. 2:3–4).

Daniel's prophecy is similar to the prophecy Jesus gave in Matthew 24 when the disciples asked when these things would take place. Jesus said the temple would be torn down and not one stone would be left on another: "Truly I say to you, not one stone shall be left here upon another that shall not be thrown down" (Matt. 24:2).

Jesus was speaking of a preview event that would occur over thirty years later. Roman troops stormed Jerusalem under the leadership of a general named Titus, who later became the emperor. During his rampage he destroyed both the Jews and their holy city. He burned Jerusalem and tore down the temple block by block so that not one block was left intact of the once-magnificent temple. It's interesting to note that during this murderous campaign, not one Christian suffered death.[12] Why? Because they heeded the words of Jesus and left Jerusalem and fled to the mountains: "When you see Jerusalem surrounded by armies, then you know that its desolation has drawn near. Then let those who are in Judea flee to the mountains, and let those who are in the city depart, and let not those who are in the country enter it" (Luke 21:20–21).

The Coming Imposter

Gabriel told Daniel that the future world leader, the "prince who shall come," will be of the same people that destroyed Jerusalem in AD 70. From this I am quite certain there will be a revival of the old Roman Empire in some shape or form (Dan. 7:7–8; 9:26–27). Remember, the Roman Empire was never overthrown and never ended but rather faded away. It will make a spectacular comeback that will cause the people of the world to adore the man who, through charm and satanic deception, made the Roman Empire reappear, seemingly overnight.

The prophets gave this man various titles, including the man of sin, the lawless one, and the son of perdition. He will be empowered by Satan and will serve as a counterfeit Christ (2 Thess. 2:1–12; Rev. 13:1–2). Gabriel calls him a "desolator" in Daniel 9:27. We will study the Antichrist's personality and policies later. This deceiver and international problem solver will project a magnetic personality. Amid the wars and rumors of war surrounding the nation of Israel and the Middle East, he will find a way to make a peace agreement between Israel and the Muslim nations—at least some of them—for seven years (equivalent to one Hebrew *shabua*): "And he shall make a firm covenant with many for one week" (Dan. 9:27). Seven is exactly the number of missing years in the prophetic calendar, the 490 years determined upon Israel's people and Holy City. The first 483 years were fulfilled when Jesus died and rose. Now the missing seven years will appear. The confirmation of this peace covenant will signal that the final *shabua*, the final seven years of human government, has begun.

Something Global, Dramatic, and Irreversible

But something else must happen to close the parenthetical period called the age of grace or the church age. That "something" will be instantaneous, astonishing, worldwide, and irreversible. Paul told us there is coming a day when the fullness of the Gentiles will arrive and the Jewish hardening toward their Messiah will begin to crack. The Rapture of the church will likely take place months prior to the

signing of the peace agreement, although we cannot say that dogmati-
cally. The world then will enter a transitional period just prior to the
final seven years. Paul wrote, "For I do not want you to be ignorant
of this mystery, brothers, lest you be wise in your own estimation,
for a partial hardening has come upon Israel until the fullness of the
Gentiles has come in" (Rom. 11:25).

This means that one day, perhaps very soon, the last Gentile will
come to Jesus Christ, completing the "fullness of the Gentiles," and
instantly the church age will be over. The church will be removed
from the earth to be with Jesus! This is the blessed hope (Titus 2:13).

After this event the world will be shaken (Heb. 12:26–27), then will
enter a transitional period leading to a unique global order. When the
seven-year peace agreement is signed and confirmed with Israel, the
Palestinians, Muslim nations, and others, the final countdown will
have begun and the world will enter the final *shabua* before Christ
returns as King of kings and Lord of lords.

Daniel 9 tells us more: "But in the middle of the week he shall
cause the sacrifice and the offering to cease. And on the wing of
abominations shall come one who makes desolate, until the decreed
destruction is poured out on the desolator" (v. 27).

In the middle of the week means after three and a half years, or
forty-two months. This is confirmed by other scriptures, including
Revelation 13:5: "He was given a mouth speaking great things and
blasphemies. And he was given authority to wage war for forty-two
months."

The final *shabua* is divided into two sections. More is written about
the final seven years—and especially the final forty-two months—
than any other prophetic period. This final *shabua* is called by different names, each describing the agony of that period. Jesus referred
to the time after the abomination of desolation as "Great Tribulation":

> For then will be great tribulation, such as has not happened
> since the beginning of the world until now, no, nor ever
> shall be.

Jeremiah called the final *shabua* "the time of Jacob's trouble," indicating there will be one final holocaust for the Jewish people (Jer. 30:7). The angel described the final seven years to Daniel as "a time of trouble such as never was since there was a nation even to that time" (Dan. 12:1). The apostle John called it "the hour of temptation which shall come upon the entire world" (Rev. 3:10).

The final seven years will be filled with sorrows and deep anguish. Those years will turn into the greatest bloodbath in history. Twenty-one rapid-fire judgments will strike the earth relentlessly, one after another (Rev. 6–19). There will be no place to hide.

In the middle of the final seven years, this prince, the world leader, will betray the peace agreement and move his own image into the holy of holies in the temple, claiming that he himself is God (2 Thess. 2:3–4). The Jews will then begin to face another holocaust of epic proportions (Zech. 13:8).

The General Prophetic Chronology of End-Time Events

As we can already see, Bible prophecy has a God-ordained order. While we don't know the precise timing of all prophetic events, we can know the general schedule and why things are happening. God gave us His prophetic Word so we can understand what will happen in the future.

The following chronology will be helpful in showing the order in which prophetic events will occur. Parts of it are flexible. For example, the Ezekiel 38 invasion of Israel could occur before or after the Rapture. Even before the Rapture we could see preliminary signs pointing to future events.

With this chronology we get a picture of God's prophetic agenda in the last days. A precise timeline is difficult, but we can get a fairly clear idea of the main events yet to come. Notice that the first six events have already happened, and we are experiencing the seventh and eighth now:

1. God promised 490 years of His prophetic dealings with Israel and the Jewish people (Dan. 9:24).

2. God promised the Messiah would come 483 years after the command to rebuild Jerusalem (Dan. 9:25–26).

3. The command to rebuild Jerusalem was issued by King Artaxerxes (Ezra 7:7–8).

4. Exactly 483 years later Jesus rode into Jerusalem on the colt of a donkey, allowing public worship of Him as Messiah for the first time. Jesus was executed, rose from the dead, and sent the Holy Spirit upon His disciples.

5. The world entered the church age, the mystery parenthetical age (Matt. 16:18–19; 1 Pet. 2:9).

6. Israel was regathered when Jews migrated from the nations to their ancient land. For the end-time prophecies to be fulfilled, Israel had to be a nation again. That happened May 14, 1948. The last days have begun! (See Isaiah 66:8; Jeremiah 31:8; Ezekiel 20:34.)

7. Preliminary signs pointing to the coming final *shabua* intensify (Luke 21:11, 25, 28).

8. Apostasy, deception, false prophets, lawlessness, and hypocrisy accelerate (Matt. 24:4, 23–26; 2 Thess. 2:3; 2 Tim. 4:3).

9. Terrorist groups are dealt a severe blow, probably by Israeli defense forces (Ps. 83).

10. A serious, perhaps nuclear, crisis unfolds in southwestern Iran (Jer. 49:34–38).

11. Damascus, Syria, is destroyed (Isa. 17).

12. Israel is invaded by Russia and Islamic allies, but God performs miracles on Israel's behalf (Ezek. 38–39). Bible commentators differ on the timing. It may happen before or after the Rapture.

13. The bride of Christ, the church, is caught away. Nobody except the Father knows when this event will happen. It is typically referred to as the Rapture (1 Cor. 15:51–55; 1 Thess. 4:13–18). This could happen without any advance notice and may happen before numbers 9–12 in this chronology.

14. The church is gone from earth and living with Christ (1 Thess. 4:16–17). Since we do not find scriptural mention of the church on Earth after Revelation 3 until we return with Jesus in Revelation 19, we may conclude the Church Age reached its completion in the event known as the Rapture (Rev. 4:1–19:14).

15. There is a resurgence of the Roman Empire (Dan. 2:41–43; 7:24; Rev. 12:3; 13:1; 17:3).

16. The United States dramatically weakens as a new multiregion federation in Europe mounts after a time of European chaos (Dan. 7:7; Rev. 17:3, 7, 12).

17. The meteoric rise of a popular and magnetic but satanic world leader occurs (2 Thess. 2:7–12; 1 John 2:18).

18. A peace treaty (covenant) is established, signed, and confirmed between Israel, Muslim nations, and other nations (Dan. 9:27).

19. The first half of time known as the Tribulation (the final *shabua*) begins (Dan. 12:1; Matt. 24:21).

20. The Jewish temple is erected in Jerusalem (Rev. 11:1–2).

21. A total of 144,000 Jewish converts emerge as impressive evangelists for Jesus Christ (Rev. 7:4–8; 14:1).

22. Judgments on earth begin to intensify (Rev. 6–19). Millions will die from war, hunger, persecution, epidemics, and geophysical changes.

23. World religions accelerate into apostasy, blending into a "harlot" religion (Rev. 17:1–6).

24. Anti-Semitism reaches a peak beyond anything in the past. During Hitler's genocidal rampage, 40 percent of the world's Jewish population was killed.[13] Under the Antichrist system, two out of every three will die (Zech. 13:8–9).

25. The Antichrist and his public relations man (a powerful and global religious leader) introduce a new economic society involving a "mark" on the right hand or forehead rather than cash (Rev. 13:16–18).

26. The Antichrist moves his image into the temple and claims to be God. His religious promoter is "allowed to give breath to the image." From this exact point there will be forty-two months until Christ's visible return (2 Thess. 2:4; Rev. 13:13–15).

27. Two supernatural prophets arise in Jerusalem (Rev. 11:3–12).

28. The second half of the Tribulation begins with increased disasters, calamities, and judgments pouring out rapidly; death camps are established for those who disagree with the Antichrist (Rev. 13–19). By this time, based on today's population, 3.7 billion will have already died, and things will get worse as the final forty-two months ensue.

29. The final scene at Armageddon takes place (Joel 3:1–3, 9–16; Zech. 14:1–4, 12; Rev. 16:12–16; 19:11–21).

30. Christ returns and is visible to the world. This is the Second Coming (Zech. 14:3, 5, 12; Rev. 19:11–16, 19).

31. The nations are judged by Christ. The Antichrist and his False Prophet/promoter are thrown into the lake of fire, along with all who took their mark of loyalty (Jer. 23:5; Matt. 25:31–46; Rev. 19–20).

32. Satan is bound for one thousand years (Rev. 20:1–3).

33. The millennial kingdom is established on earth for precisely one thousand years with Jesus Himself ruling from Jerusalem (Isa. 2:2–4; 11:6–9; 65:20–22; Zech. 8:22–23; Rev. 20:4–6).

34. Satan is loosed for a final short season after the thousand years to test those humans not resurrected and their descendants who remained on the earth after Christ returned. A final rebellion will ensue (Rev. 20:7–10).

35. The second resurrection (for the damned) takes place after the thousand years, when those in Hades (hell's holding place) reunite with their bodies and are raised to attend the great white throne judgment. All Christ rejecters will be declared guilty and banished forever (Rev. 20:11–15).

36. A new heaven and new earth with New Jerusalem as the capital city are established forever (Rev. 21:1–27).

An Exciting Project

I would like to suggest a project that will be valuable in your understanding of God's agenda for the future. It will cause hope and faith to surge forth inside of you. Repeatedly read these portions of Scripture, which give a clear picture of the prophetic chronology. You won't need my commentary or anyone else's. As you read these scriptures over and over, like adjusting a camera lens, everything will come into sharper focus as the Holy Spirit reveals the future to you (John 16:13).

Again, you don't need to be a prophecy expert to understand the last days! Enjoy the following Scripture passages and study them again and again.

+ Daniel 2

+ Daniel 7

+ Daniel 9

+ Daniel 12

+ Matthew 24–25

+ Mark 13

+ 1 Thessalonians

+ 2 Thessalonians

+ Revelation

Having laid out the approximate prophetic chronology, let's briefly look at the final prophetic book of the New Testament and learn how to unravel it.

Decoding the Apocalypse

Let's move now to the Apocalypse. The Book of Revelation—the Apocalypse—is the final book of the Bible, a culmination of biblical prophecies. Its cryptic style and mysterious symbols have left many shaking their heads, dismissing the book as impossible to understand. But if that's the case, why would the Holy Spirit ensure that John recorded it? Several times in this book we read, "He who has an ear, let him hear what the Spirit says to the churches" (e.g., Rev. 2:7). God meant for us to read and hear the writings of the Book of Revelation and promised a blessing for those who do (Rev. 1:3).

We are told in the first verse of Revelation that Jesus Himself sent this revelation by "His angel," who "signified" these things. *Signified* means "made known by signs." Many clues to properly decoding the Apocalypse are found in Revelation 1:

1. Much of the Revelation will be in cryptic signs (v. 1).

2. John was writing what he saw: "What you see, write in a book" (v. 11). We must understand, John was seeing the present, the future, the spirit world, the natural world, and various geographical locations. All of these include personalities and events that will occur in the future. We need the assistance of the Holy Spirit and other scriptures to help us determine, for example, if John was writing about something he was seeing in the natural world or something of the spiritual realm.

    Study to show yourself approved by God, a workman who need not be ashamed, rightly dividing the word of truth.
    —2 Timothy 2:15

    As you read the Apocalypse, ask, "Was John seeing the spirit world or natural world in this passage? What is the event taking place here? Where could it happen? Where else in Scripture is this term used?"

3. Remember, Scripture interprets Scripture. If there is a symbol used in Revelation, it will be used somewhere else in Scripture to identify and determine the meaning.

In chapters 1–3 we see a sketch of the past and present. Chapters 2 and 3 depict the church age, offering many spiritual and practical insights for the church today. Chapter 4 begins the future. John wrote, "After this I looked. And there was an open door in heaven. The first voice I heard was like a trumpet speaking with me, saying, 'Come up here, and I will show you things which must take place after this'" (v. 1). John wrote the words "after this" twice in this verse. So we ask, "After what?" It's after chapters 2 and 3, depicting the church age. What follows in chapters 4–22 are future events occurring *after* the end of the church age.

Another thing to note is this: when you read words such as "must soon take place" (e.g., Rev. 1:1), they mean that once the events of Revelation begin, they will be rapid-fire. When you read, "I am coming soon" (e.g., Rev. 22:7), it's speaking of imminence; Jesus's return could happen at any moment. A good outline of Revelation would look like this:

+ Chapter 1: Introduction and explanations

+ Chapters 2–3: Church age

+ Chapters 4–5: Church in heaven and transition period on earth

+ Chapters 6–19: Tribulation on earth (final *shabua*, last seven years of mankind's own ways) and Jesus Christ's triumphant return

+ Chapter 20: Millennial kingdom and final judgment

+ Chapter 21: New heaven and new earth

+ Chapter 22: Final appeal to come to Jesus Christ before it's too late

Now read the Book of Revelation in a whole new way and enjoy the Holy Spirit as He blesses you with more pieces of the prophetic puzzle.

Chapter 5

PREVIEW SIGNS OF THE APOCALYPSE

A SNEAK PEEK INTO THE FUTURE

So also, when you shall see all these things,
you know that it is near, even at the doors.
—JESUS, MATTHEW 24:33

WHY DO I believe we are most likely the generation that will see the coming of Christ? Because of the massive convergence of precise signs, specific markers, and categorical conditions God laid out for us long ago that point toward the return of Jesus. We may now be experiencing what the Bible calls "birth pangs" (Matt. 24:8, AMP). Woe to us if we ignore these signs!

Don't Ignore the Signals

I almost ignored important signs one Sunday night when I was preaching. My pregnant wife started having intense contractions, though I didn't realize it at the time. Ladies of the church gathered around her in one of the back pews, trying to signal me as they pointed to Mary Jo's belly and then pointed to their watches. I tried not to pay any attention because I wanted to finish my sermon.

Immediately following the altar call, I rushed Mary Jo to the hospital. The nurse scolded me: "Mr. Williams, you didn't get her here any too soon. She's already at eight centimeters!" I didn't know what "eight centimeters" meant, but I knew she was trying to tell me I should have brought my wife sooner. Mary Jo's contractions became more intense and more frequent, signaling that the baby was about to be born. Not long after that, our beautiful daughter entered the world.

When Jesus wanted to describe what the beginning of sorrows would be like, he used the picture of birth pangs or contractions. They are not pleasant, but they signal that the birth is about to take place.

> But all these things are *merely* the beginning of birth pangs.
> —Matthew 24:8, amp

All the signs Jesus foretold in Matthew 24 and Mark 13—these birth pangs or global contractions—point to the world's final era of unprecedented trouble, the Tribulation. This is what I have been calling the final *shabua*. The Bible gives no specific signs for when the Rapture of the church will take place. It could happen at any moment without warning or any preconditions. Yet when we study the forecasted conditions on earth leading up to the Tribulation, we can easily discern the season and the times (1 Thess. 5:1–3) by these birth pangs of which Jesus spoke. In fact, we are supposed to! Jesus rebuked the hypocritical religious leaders for not discerning the prophetic signs:

> When it is evening, you say, "It will be fair weather, for the sky is red," and in the morning, "It will be foul weather today, for the sky is red and overcast." O you hypocrites, you can discern the face of the sky, but you cannot discern the signs of the times.
> —Matthew 16:2–3

We are now seeing the signs, conditions, and markers falling into place in preparation for the dreaded hour of agony. Those who refuse to surrender to the only Savior given to mankind, Jesus Christ, and insist on being their own god will experience a frightening and dreadful future. But God loves the world enough to post signs so we need not be deceived concerning the perilous hour in which we live. Beware—the small deceptions of today will become the grand delusions of tomorrow!

> Therefore God will send them a strong delusion, that they should believe the lie: that they all might be condemned who did not believe the truth but had pleasure in unrighteousness.
>
> —2 THESSALONIANS 2:11–12

Preview Signs

I call the preliminary signs "preview signs" because they preview coming events. They will reach their fulfillment during the Tribulation (described in detail in Revelation 6–19), becoming no longer just previews but real judgments on a God-hating, Christ-rejecting world.

My wife and I were returning from Hawaii to Los Angeles recently, and as we flew over the Pacific Ocean at night, we saw something we had never seen before. It looked like hundreds of stars were falling out of the sky. The captain explained to us that it was a predicted meteor shower and would be of no danger to us. It wasn't a prophetic sign of anything, but it did remind me of Jesus's prophecies that one day "the stars will fall from heaven, and the powers of the heavens will be shaken" (Matt. 24:29), and "there will be signs in the sun and the moon and the stars; and on the earth distress of nations, with perplexity, the sea and the waves roaring" (Luke 21:25).

Signs can be minor or major. A harbinger is a sign that is much stronger than a blinking light. A harbinger is a serious and sobering real-time glimpse into what will follow in a more dramatic manner if a nation or individual refuses to repent and turn back to God.

When we see the multiple signs Jesus spoke of concerning the last days, we know the hour is approaching. Once the hour strikes, there is no turning back. It will occur suddenly with no more time to prepare.

> You know perfectly that the day of the Lord will come like a thief in the night.
>
> —1 THESSALONIANS 5:2

> The day of the Lord will come like a thief in the night.
>
> —2 PETER 3:10

Once the final *shabua* begins, the rapid-fire judgments will be relentless. Some refer to this as Judgment Day. Sadly for those on earth, Judgment Day will last much longer than a day. It will continue for seven years, with the severest and most brutal events taking place in the final three-and-a-half-year period, which Jesus called the Great Tribulation.

Blinkers and Lights

When you see someone's car blinker on, you know the car is going to turn. If they flash their headlights at you, you know you either have your high beams on or maybe it's nighttime and your lights are off. In other words, we are accustomed to reading signals all day long.

The year 2015 brought an aggregation of "blinkers" in the heavens, including Comet Lovejoy (C/2014 Q2) with its pale green color. An unusual tetrad of four blood moons ended in 2015. Then a surprise blood moon, caused by smoke from forest fires, appeared over the United States and parts of Canada, occurring right after the Supreme Court's decision to redefine marriage.[1] The Star of Bethlehem appeared in the constellation Leo, though it attracted little secular press; a rare convergence of Venus and Jupiter brought the phenomenon, with the bright star Regulus aligning with the planets.[2] It's rare that so many cosmic events happen in such close succession. I recall casually reading a secular blog that mentioned the heavenly sights, and the writer, out of the blue, asked the question, "Is God trying to tell us something?" Not a bad observation!

Beheadings

The terrorist attacks and brutal beheadings in the Middle East are live-action harbingers of what is to come globally unless we humble ourselves, pray, turn from our wicked ways, and seek God with all of our hearts (2 Chron. 7:14). During the coming Tribulation, beheadings will increase exponentially: "And I saw the souls of those who had been beheaded for their witness of Jesus and for the word of God" (Rev. 20:4).

Water Contamination

In Flint, Michigan, a water contamination crisis began in 2014 when the city changed its water supply from Lake Huron and the Detroit River to the Flint River in an effort to save money. But apparently the water (or water piping) was not properly treated, which led to serious contamination. Reports surfaced of children's hair falling out and people developing serious health issues from water that contained lead and other heavy metals.[3]

The last report I read indicated that six thousand to twelve thousand children were exposed to the contaminated drinking water and now may face a series of lifelong health issues.[4] Can you imagine being a parent of one of these children exposed to the polluted water?

Contaminated water is also a possible cause of an outbreak of Legionnaires' disease in Genesee County (where Flint is located) that has killed ten people and affected another seventy-seven.[5]

This is what it will be like for millions during the Tribulation when one-third of the earth's fresh water supply becomes polluted with deadly toxins (Rev. 8:10–11). The Flint water crisis is not the biblical event, but it is a preview sign of what is coming for those who have rejected God's call of love.

Euphrates River Drying Up

Four predominantly Muslim nations sit on the Euphrates: Iraq, Syria, Turkey, and a small portion of Iran (on the Shatt al-Arab, formed by the convergence of the Euphrates and Tigris Rivers). By early 2015 the Islamic State (ISIS) had captured strategic positions along the Euphrates. The Bible speaks of this region:

> The sixth angel sounded, and I heard a voice from the four horns of the golden altar which is before God, saying to the sixth angel who had the trumpet, "Release the four angels who are bound at the great Euphrates River." And the four

angels, who had been prepared for the hour and day and month and year, were released to kill a third of mankind.

—Revelation 9:13–15

The sixth angel poured out his bowl on the great Euphrates River, and its water was dried up, to prepare the way for the kings from the East.

—Revelation 16:12

Several news outlets reported in 2015 and 2016 that the Euphrates River is drying up.[6] Not only has the Euphrates River suffered diminishing water levels over the past ten years, but ISIS began using water as a weapon in 2014 by taking control of the Mosul Dam.[7]

The drying up of the Euphrates has produced other consequences. Desert horned vipers are fleeing the river as it dries up. The deadly vipers have become a plague among the people living near the river. Doctors in the area say people are being killed by the snakes, and people are leaving their homes out of fear.[8]

Is this prophecy a fulfillment of Revelation 16? No, but it's certainly a birth pang signaling what the final fulfillment will be like during the Tribulation.

Violence

Jesus warned, "As were the days of Noah, so will be the coming of the Son of Man" (Matt. 24:37). What was it like during the days of Noah? "The earth was corrupt before God and filled with violence" (Gen. 6:11).

The violence that brought destruction to the earth in Noah's day is the same condition we see today. Think about the terms that have become so common in just the past decade: domestic violence, ethnic violence, police violence, school violence, workplace violence.

We experienced a bombardment of news about police shootings, race clashes, and protests after the 2016 presidential election, which turned violent. We witnessed shocking news clips of a man being beaten on the street because he voted for Donald Trump.[9]

Months earlier we watched in horror as we saw twenty-one Christian men dressed in orange jumpsuits being herded to the shoreline of the Mediterranean, where radical Islamists gleefully hacked their heads off.[10] These twenty-one Coptic Christians were only looking for work when ISIS members violently seized them and determined their fate. These men were innocent sons, dads, brothers, and husbands who would never return home to their families because of bloodthirsty violence. We felt compassion for the heartbroken, grieving families as their images flashed across our computer screens and television sets.[11]

And how can we ever forget the gruesome video of the caged Jordanian pilot doused with gasoline and brutally burned alive? His screams and cries as he fell to his knees will forever ring in our minds as we mourn for his family and loved ones.[12]

Now, in America, the FBI has confirmed that violent crime is once again on the rise.[13] But violence is not limited to harming people physically. There are those who violate others by selling shabby products that don't work. That is a form of violence. Identity theft is violence. Imagine receiving bills for purchases you didn't make or being convicted of crimes you didn't commit. It happened to a man in Texas, and it's happening to others.[14]

"So God said to Noah, 'The end of all flesh is come before Me, for the earth is filled with violence because of them. Now I will destroy them with the earth'" (Gen. 6:13).

Famines, Epidemics, and Earthquakes

> For nation will rise against nation, and kingdom against kingdom. There will be famines, epidemics, and earthquakes in various places.
> —MATTHEW 24:7

NBC News did a news piece on the worldwide surge in what they classified as "great" earthquakes.[15] Today there is a website exclusively devoted to helping us keep up with all the seismic activity.[16] *USA Today* reported about some of the deadliest earthquakes in the past decade. Here is just a sampling: December 26, 2004—230,000 dead in Indonesia; October 8, 2005—80,000 dead in Pakistan; May 12, 2008—nearly 90,000 dead in China; January 12, 2010—316,000 dead in Haiti; March 11, 2011—18,000 dead or missing in Japan; and April 25, 2015—more than 8,000 dead in Nepal.[17]

We have all watched television reports of deadly pestilences and famines in places such as Ethiopia, Sudan, and other spots around the world. Epidemics in the Bible were sometimes called "pestilences." This word can refer to deadly diseases or figuratively to pests, such as mosquitoes.[18] The last decade has produced its share of news about pestilences, including the deadly Ebola outbreak in West Africa. The Centers for Disease Control tries to keep the evolving issue under close investigation.[19] A *Washington Post* article from November 2016 blasted this headline: "The Ebola Outbreak May Have Been Bigger Than Believed."[20]

The Florida Department of Health is tracking the Zika virus, known to cause deforming birth defects when pregnant women are infected.[21] As of December 19, 2016, there were 194 pregnant women in Florida with lab evidence of being infected.[22] Can you imagine the panic and despair these families must be feeling? This could be a great opportunity for believers to intervene and pray with these families for a miracle. It seems that God loves to work miracles that point people to His Son and bring them into the faith.

Wars and Rumors of War

Jesus foretold that "nation will rise against nation" (Matt. 24:7; Mark 13:8; Luke 21:10). The Greek word for "nation" is *ethnos*, from which our English word *ethnic* is derived. Ethnic groups will rise against each other and try to remove each other from a particular territory. This is happening today in Iraq, Syria, and Libya at the hands of Islamic jihadists against Christians, Yazidis, Shiite Muslims, and anyone else deemed an infidel. Ethnic cleansing has occurred throughout history, but the past century has seen an unprecedented acceleration. The Nazi Holocaust annihilated six million European Jews in an ethnic cleansing attempt. Forced displacement and mass killings in the former Yugoslavia and in the African country of Rwanda during the 1990s highlighted again these words of Jesus. The world is experiencing an era of ethnic rage, a preview sign of what is to come.

I mentioned earlier that the Middle East would be the world's end-time focal point. Syria is in severe crisis as a result of civil war, and Russia's involvement may not be helping. Eleven million people have been forced from their homes and a quarter of a million have died in the conflict.[23] Iran is allegedly on the path to nuclear weapons. Iraq continues its efforts to drive out the Islamic State. Turkey faced a failed coup in 2016 and seems to be shifting to more of a dictatorship under President Recep Tayyip Erdoğan.[24]

So, here we are: the Middle Eastern world is dominating the spotlight, just as was forecast by the ancient prophets.

The Sign of Israel Blinks Strong

One biblical sign blinks brighter than all the others: God's promise to return the Jews in the last days to the same homeland the Romans expelled them from in AD 70.

> In that day the Lord shall set His hand again the second time to recover the remnant of His people, who shall be left, from Assyria, from Egypt, from Pathros, from Cush, from Elam, from Shinar, from Hamath, and from the islands of the sea.
>
> He shall set up a banner for the nations, and shall assemble the outcasts of Israel, and gather together the dispersed of Judah from the four corners of the earth.
>
> —Isaiah 11:11–12

> For surely the days are coming, says the Lord, when I will restore the fortunes of My people Israel and Judah. The Lord says, I also will cause them to return to the land that I gave to their fathers, and they shall possess it.
>
> —Jeremiah 30:3

After many days you shall be called. In the latter years you shall come into the land that is restored from the sword, whose inhabitants have been gathered out of many peoples, against the mountains of Israel which had been always a waste. But its people were brought out of the nations, and they, all of them, are dwelling safely.

—EZEKIEL 38:8

The very existence of Israel as a nation today cannot be underestimated as a powerful sign of the days we are living in. I consider it by far the greatest sign that these are the end times.

Silence and Darkness

During the US presidential debates of 2016, one presidential candidate addressed the potential of an EMP (electromagnetic pulse) attack on the United States.[25] An EMP attack could wipe out a nation's electrical grid, all electronics, all vehicles with electronic systems, and all electric pumps, creating literal silence and darkness.

Sit silently, and go into darkness, O daughter of the Chaldeans; for you shall no more be called the queen of kingdoms.

—ISAIAH 47:5

An electromagnetic pulse can result from a mammoth, out-of-the-ordinary solar flare. It can also be humanly caused by detonating a nuclear device at a high altitude above the target nation. With North Korea, under the radical and unstable rule of Kim Jong Un, in possession of nuclear weapons, an EMP attack against the United States is certainly in the realm of possibility. In fact, CNN reported on March 28, 2016, that North Korea threatened war with the United States in a propaganda video.[26]

In the Book of Revelation we are told that during the Tribulation the world will not only experience spiritual darkness but literal darkness (8:12; 16:10). How can darkness come to a nation in a nanosecond? An EMP attack over a particular nation is certainly one possibility.

Imagine that you and your spouse decide to take a vacation far from home. You have grown children and grandchildren, and you are now retired. Suddenly a solar flare or an explosion over your location brings an electromagnetic pulse that completely neutralizes batteries, electronic equipment, cell phones, electronic notebooks, and everything that has anything to do with electronics. There is no radio, television, phone service, or Internet, and no vehicles are moving. What are you going to do? How can you get back home?

An EMP event would devastate any country. It would take months or even years to get communications and transportation back up and running. With Iran on the path to nuclear capabilities and with a stated agenda to destroy Western civilization as well as Israel, this scenario could be getting closer.

Unresolvable National Problems

Not long ago Franklin Graham posted on his Facebook page: "The Bible tells us that in the end times there will be 'distress of nations with perplexity.' This is certainly the case today.... Israel is desperate to have peace, but the Bible says 'they will seek peace but there shall be none.' There is only one ultimate, eternal solution—Jesus Christ and Him alone."[27]

Reverend Graham was quoting what Jesus prophesied would occur in the last days just before His coming: "distress of nations, with perplexity" (Luke 21:25). *Perplexity* describes our culture today. Luke 21:25 has the only occurrence of this word, *aporia*, in the Bible. It is related to anxiety or puzzlement. The Oxford Dictionary defines *aporia* as "an irresolvable internal contradiction or logical disjunction in a text, argument, or theory."[28] I'm drawn to that word *irresolvable*. It seems to define our day. I'm certain a thrust for a global government will be man's attempt to resolve these "irresolvable" problems. But the only real and effective solution is in turning back to the living God.

In America national debt is squeezing the life out of our nation. Some economists say that not only US debt but also global debt is now reaching "terminal velocity," which means a global financial collapse may be right around the corner.[29]

In so many arenas of life, people have questions but no good earthly answers. Thankfully believers possess promises from God. We are absolutely confident that the Lord knows what He is doing, even when we are facing seemingly unsolvable problems. The apostle Paul said confidently, "Be anxious for nothing, but in everything, by prayer and supplication with gratitude, make your requests known to God" (Phil. 4:6).

We should have no anxiety over the perplexity of the world. Even when Jesus was giving the signs of the coming Tribulation, He made a point of telling believers, "See that you are not troubled" (Matt. 24:6).

Attacks on the Truth

When the disciples asked Jesus about His coming and signs of the end of the age, the first thing Jesus warned them about was the attack on truth that would prevail in the last days: "Take heed that no one deceives you" (Matt. 24:4).

Deception is a powerful sign and birth pang. Today a cloud of confusion blankets our world. Chaos seems the order of the day. Confusion and deception permeate our economy, the political world, the religious world, and everywhere else. Everything is becoming increasingly complicated. Even the term *evangelical* has lost its meaning with the emergence of the "new evangelicals" who sound more like socialists than Christians.[30] Faulty theology is leading to dangerous positions on the wrong side of God's boundaries.

The world is rapidly being prepared through deception for the appearance of the supreme deception of this age, the dreaded Antichrist. *Deception* is defined in the Greek language as "roaming" or "wandering." The word suggests that a deceived person has been seduced or taken off course. Deception is always an undercover strategy of the enemy. The victim does not realize he or she is a target. Like a good animal trap, deception is hidden until it is too late for the victim to escape. There are no flags flying above the land mines of deception. Traps are hidden, and the person drifting into deception does not recognize that he or she is being seduced.

Deception always begins in the heart as a result of honoring one's personal will above the will of almighty God. The will of man by nature does not love the truth. In their unrepentant state, people willingly trade God's truth for satanic lies—and the consequences are devastating.

> The lawless one will be revealed…even him, whose coming is in accordance with the working of Satan with all power and signs and false wonders, and with all deception of unrighteousness among those who perish, because they did not receive the love for the truth that they might be saved. Therefore God will send them a strong delusion, that they should believe the lie: that they all might be condemned who did not believe the truth but had pleasure in unrighteousness.
> —2 Thessalonians 2:8–12

> For the time will come when people will not endure sound doctrine, but they will gather to themselves teachers in accordance with their own desires, having itching ears, and they will turn their ears away from the truth and turn to myths.
> —2 Timothy 4:3–4

Most troubling to me are the false teachers within professing Christianity. Some still call themselves "evangelical" yet have renounced fundamental doctrines such as the virgin birth of Jesus, the doctrine of hell, and the belief that the Bible is the inspired Word of God.

> For such are false apostles and deceitful workers, disguising themselves as apostles of Christ. And no wonder! For even Satan disguises himself as an angel of light. Therefore it is no great thing if his ministers also disguise themselves as

ministers of righteousness, whose end will be according to
their works.

—2 Corinthians 11:13–15

Where is this deception leading? It's heading toward a world conglomerate religion during the Tribulation. (See 2 Thessalonians 2:3–4;
Revelation 17:1–6.) We see dramatic signs of this religion forming
now. The only way Satan can pull off this deception is by convincing
churchgoing people that the Bible is inspired only in certain spots, or
that only the words of Jesus are exclusively inspired, or that there is
no hell and we shouldn't preach about it, or that all religions worship
the same God, or all of the above. He is attempting to do this now
through articulate spokesmen and winsome representatives of a false
gospel.

We are seeing a huge escalation of what can only be labeled "strong
delusion." Some so-called scholars are saying hell is a pagan religious
concept that Christians have stolen as a doctrine. Some believe that
all religions lead to God. I have known ministers who teach that
"everybody is saved; only they don't know it." You can believe these
deceptions if you want, but the eternal consequences will be severe.

Some professing Christians are saying, "Islam is good and peaceful,"
even though they know what the Islamic religion does to women and
"infidels." Others suggest that guns are the problem, and they recommend making guns illegal, even for good citizens. Some political
candidates actually say that climate change is more dangerous than
terrorism.[31]

Delusion is deepening as we approach the coming of Christ—and
this is a major sign of the times.

The apostle Paul grieved over those who placed pleasure over God's
truth. First, they will come under a strong delusion and believe the
lie of the coming world leader—the Antichrist (2 Thess. 2:11). Second,
they will be condemned to face the world's greatest hour of agony—
the final *shabua* (Dan. 12:1; Matt. 24:21; Rev. 6–19). Third, they will
have no hope of escaping the horrors of the place prepared for Satan
and his followers (Matt. 23:33; 25:41; Luke 16:23; 2 Pet. 2:1–10; Rev.

19:20; 20:10). But Paul rejoiced and thanked God for those who believe the truth and have been called by the Spirit of God to salvation and sanctification (2 Thess. 2:13).

Christianity—true Christianity—is exclusive. Jesus said, "I am the way, the truth, and the life. No one comes to the Father except through Me" (John 14:6). The apostle Peter warned, "There is no salvation in any other, for there is no other name under heaven given among men by which we must be saved" (Acts 4:12). And Paul wrote of a God "who desires all men to be saved and to come to the knowledge of the truth. There is one God and one mediator between God and men, the Man Christ Jesus, who gave Himself as a ransom for all" (1 Tim. 2:4–6).

Jesus reminded His listeners, "Enter at the narrow gate, for wide is the gate and broad is the way that leads to destruction, and there are many who are going through it, because small is the gate and narrow is the way which leads to life, and there are few who find it" (Matt. 7:13–14).

Pastors must rise up against the antichrist spirit and explain the truth of God in simple, effective ways. Teach verse by verse so the flock will grow in the grace and knowledge of the Lord Jesus and His plan for these last days. Pastor, please don't be afraid to preach the gospel of Jesus Christ and the gospel of the kingdom. The hour is late. The final roundup has begun, and God will use you as His agent— His ambassador—to bring in a great harvest of souls, rescuing them from hell's grip.

> He has delivered us from the power of darkness and has transferred us into the kingdom of His dear Son, in whom we have redemption through His blood, the forgiveness of sins.
>
> —COLOSSIANS 1:13–14

Hell was never prepared for humans, but for Satan and his forces. Jesus died on the cross to keep people out of that place and to give them a new nature. Yet people choose to go there rather than follow

Jesus Christ, God's Son. Jesus will say to them, "Depart from Me, you cursed, into the eternal fire, prepared for the devil and his angels" (Matt. 25:41).

Concerning the preview signs, Jesus said, "When these things begin to happen, look up and lift up your heads, for your redemption is drawing near" (Luke 21:28). When you see the previews of coming attractions, you know the main feature will soon begin. We are seeing many previews that signal that the main feature is just about to begin. Let's get ready for it, spiritually, attitudinally, and in practical day-to-day ways.

Chapter 6

LAST DAYS NATIONS AND GROUPS

THE CHILLING ACCURACY OF THE ANCIENT PROPHETS

> Why do the nations rage, and the peoples plot in vain? The
> kings of the earth set themselves, and the rulers take counsel
> together, against the LORD and against His anointed, saying,
> "Let us tear off their bonds and cast away their ropes from us."
> —PSALM 2:1–3

AN UNPRECEDENTED ALIGNMENT of last days nations and groups is taking place today. According to the prophets Ezekiel and Daniel, this alignment would take place in the latter times (Ezek. 38:8, 16; Dan. 2:28). The specific positioning of many of these nations and groups has never happened in history—until now.

A common practice of the ancient biblical prophets was to use the territorial names of their time to identify an end-time region or country. For example, the prophet Ezekiel would say, "Persia," which was the region we know today as Iran. This will help us in understanding how and where these prophecies will be fulfilled.

Let's dive into the ancient prophecies relating to these end-time nations and groups.

Israel

As we noted in chapter 5, Israel is the largest blinking sign that the last days have begun. Israel forms the epicenter of biblical prophecy. Remember that Israel and the church are distinct entities. In the Book of Acts alone, the church and Israel are distinguished from each other twenty different times. Romans 9–11 also makes this abundantly clear. The church did not replace Israel, as some replacement theologians proclaim today. In all end-time prophecies, Israel is back in its land under self-governance. After World War II, on May 14, 1948, the nation of Israel truly experienced a miracle rebirth, for the Jewish people had been scattered throughout other countries for more than two millennia. Nothing like it has ever happened in human history. Prophecy teachers of old told us that when the Jews were miraculously brought back to their land, we would know that we were in the last days.

Israel's journey was foretold by God, who repeatedly warned the Jewish people that they would be scattered to foreign nations if they were unfaithful to their covenant (Lev. 26:33; Deut. 28:64). But God promised that even though they would no longer possess an official homeland, He would personally preserve the Jewish people during their worldwide sojourn in other countries (Isa. 66:22). The Lord promised never to forget Israel and said that He would be like a mother who could never forget her nursing child (Isa. 49:15).

The Lord also warned the Jews that if they failed to listen to Him, they would be persecuted wherever they went (Deut. 28:65–67). Just as Moses prophesied, they were persecuted. Satan has a special hatred for the Jews. After all, God gave us the Holy Scriptures and even the Messiah, Jesus Christ, through the Jews. God loves the Jewish people, and His heart cries out for them to come to the true Jewish Messiah—and one day they will.

Since the dispersal of the Jewish people among the nations, everything the prophets said proved true. The Jews were scattered globally, suffered enormous persecution, and maintained their Jewish bloodline. This is unprecedented for any dispersed people group in all of history.

But there are more biblical prophecies concerning Israel. The Old Testament prophets repeatedly promised that a day would come when God would assemble the Jews back to their land in the last days: "For I will take you from among the nations and gather you out of all countries and will bring you into your own land" (Ezek. 36:24).

In Ezekiel 38–39 the prophet gave us a precise picture of a future event sometimes referred to as the war of Magog. This takes place "in the latter years" after Israel is a nation again (Ezek. 38:8). The prophecies of Ezekiel 38–39 could not be fulfilled in any period of history until now.

Jesus Himself gave us one of the most stunning and certain signs of His soon coming when He said the Jews would once again occupy and control Jerusalem when "the times of the Gentiles are fulfilled" (Luke 21:24). Again, this happened during the Six-Day War in June 1967.

Prophetically Israel is the key component of the future. God loves the Jewish people, continues to call them to His Son, and has never given up on them. Many Jewish people have turned to their Messiah and discovered the peace and hope Jesus Christ gives to all who come to Him. But in a general sense, the hearts of the Jewish people remain closed to their Messiah.

Here is the great news and true hope of Israel: Jesus Christ will return to earth with His bride, the church. After putting a stop to the war of all wars, Armageddon, and ending the persecution of His precious Jewish people, He will select Jerusalem to be the capital not just of Israel but of the entire world. Jesus will reign on David's throne from the city of Jerusalem during the coming thousand years of peace, order, love, and kindness (Zech. 14:9–11; Luke 1:31–33; Rev. 20:1–6). That is a great future for God's beloved nation!

European Nations

Today we are witnessing a power shift away from the United States and toward the European Union. An agenda is driving Europe toward a confederation, a United States of Europe, a kind of revival of the Roman Empire.[1] This end-time conglomeration of countries and regions is described as "dreadful and terrible, and exceedingly strong" (Dan. 7:7). As Daniel views this heavenly vision, a little horn arises from this European empire, with "eyes like the eyes of man, and a mouth speaking great things" (Dan. 7:8). This little horn describes the coming world leader, the Antichrist, and reveals how he will in some way be connected with the revived Roman Empire.

This emerging European confederation will have an enormous impact on trade and global resources, and eventually will either diminish the role of the United Nations in global affairs or completely take control of it. Today the European Union is experiencing a back-lash over Muslim immigration and terrorist acts in France, Belgium, and the United Kingdom, but this chaos may actually be the catalyst for the rising little horn, "the man with solutions."

The European Union flag includes twelve gold stars on a blue back-ground. Officially the circle of twelve stars represents "solidarity and harmony between the peoples of Europe." The number twelve is "tra-ditionally the symbol of perfection, completeness and unity." [2] This sounds eerily like the original Babel's rebellious design to defy God's instructions to disperse throughout the earth. Under the leadership of Nimrod, the people started erecting a tower in defiance of God, "lest we be scattered abroad upon the face of the whole earth" (Gen. 11:4, KJV). The tower hosted an astrological worship center designed to worship the creation rather than the Creator.

The apostle Paul reminds us that an apostate culture will again repeat the same defiance toward God and His boundaries: "They turned the truth of God into a lie and worshipped and served the creature rather than the Creator, who is blessed forever" (Rom. 1:25). God instructed men to disperse and replenish the earth, but some of Noah's descendants wanted to keep God out of their society and rule themselves, so God confused their languages to stop them. This may be an indicator that God designed for there to be separate nations, ethnicities, and people groups. The Lord never designed or approved of a global government, other than the government of His kingdom.

Interestingly the European Union issued a poster that "showed a version of the Pieter Bruegel painting of the Tower of Babel with tower cranes resuming its construction where once God had intervened to halt the work."[3] The poster carried the caption "Europe: Many Tongues One Voice." Another related note is that the European Youth Portal runs an online magazine called, of all things, *Café Babel*.[4]

The curious symbol often associated with the European Union, however, is even more interesting in light of biblical prophecy. It is a picture of a woman riding a beast. It appears on a Greek Euro coin, is seen in statues near EU buildings, and is in a mosaic in an EU Parliament building.[5] The woman, Europa, is a symbol connected to a Greek myth, later adopted by the Romans. The apostle John saw something similar in the Spirit: "I saw a woman sitting on a scarlet beast which was full of blasphemous names, having seven heads and ten horns" (Rev. 17:3).

Based on Daniel 2:41–42 and Revelation 17:9–11 many scholars believe that the headquarters of the coming global government will initially be located in Europe, the region of the old Roman Empire. "This calls for a mind with understanding: The seven heads of the beast represent the seven hills where the woman rules. They also represent seven kings" (Rev. 17:9, NLT). Rome is still called the city of seven hills. Constantinople (modern-day Istanbul, Turkey) was also named the city of seven hills by Roman emperor Constantine when he moved his headquarters there. But there are more than "seven hills" to this prophecy. John, in his vision of a woman sitting on a scarlet beast with seven heads and ten horns, wrote:

> Here is the mind which has wisdom: The seven heads are seven mountains on which the woman sits. They are also seven kings. Five have fallen, one is, the other has not yet come; and when he comes, he must remain a little while. Concerning the beast who was, and is not, he is the eighth, and is of the seven, and is going to destruction. The ten horns which you saw are ten kings who have received no kingdom yet, but they will receive authority as kings for one hour with

the beast. These are of one mind and will give their power
and authority to the beast.

—REVELATION 17:9–13

John saw the seven mountains as being seven heads and seven
kings. Of these seven kings, or seven empires, John said that five have
fallen (Egypt, Assyria, Babylonia, Medo-Persia, and Greece), one is
(speaking of the empire that still existed at the time of his writing,
Rome), and one has not yet come (revived Roman Empire). The world
historically has only had six world empires. The seventh, the revived
Roman Empire, is now arising, but its rule will be brief. The "New
Europe" may be in the midst of becoming the prophesied revived
Roman Empire, the final human empire in history.

According to New Testament prophets, the newly established
Roman kingdom of the last days will host a global government (Rev.
13:7), a syncretistic false religion represented by Mystery, Babylon the
Great (Rev. 13:14–15; 17:5), and a global cyber economy (Rev. 13:16–18).
The revived Roman Empire will produce a beloved world leader, a
man with persuasive solutions to the perplexing problems of the
world. He will end up revealing himself as the most wicked dictator
the world has ever known.

In Revelation 17:12–13 John confirms what the prophet Daniel
foretold. From Daniel 2 we know that iron represents the Roman
kingdom. From that Roman kingdom in the last days a conglomerate
of nations will form, some strong and some not so strong. Daniel
was given revelation about the final world "beast" government (Dan.
7:7–8).

The beast kingdom characterizes the future Rome. The ten horns
represent multiple leaders in this coming kingdom, three of whom
are violently conquered by the little horn (the Antichrist), perhaps
because they revolted against his leadership. We also know that the
impending European kingdom will become global (Dan. 7:23).

Watch for a dramatic power shift toward Europe. The alignment
has begun. Clearly the new world order will issue from the revived
Roman Empire.

Chaos in Europe

Willing to sacrifice economic stability for the safety of their families in light of the rapid influx of Muslim refugees, the citizens of the United Kingdom voted to leave the European Union in June 2016. The Muslim population of Europe has increased significantly in recent years[6] as large numbers of Islamic immigrants entered the European Union through Hungary and Germany. Once they were in the European Union, travel to other EU member nations became very easy under EU laws. Issues such as the ongoing crisis of sexual assault and rape by migrant refugees in Germany and talk of increasing violent crime in the United Kingdom associated with migrants put immigration issues at the forefront.[7] The common British citizens finally said, "Enough!"

"Brexit" led to citizens of other EU nations wanting out.[8] European Union leaders are angry over the United Kingdom's exit.[9] What does this mean prophetically? It means that more chaos will ensue in the area of the old Roman Empire, opening the door for a magnetic man to arise on a peace platform to bring order and security. The whole world will be impressed and marvel at him, adore him, and want him to solve the rest of the world's challenges (Rev. 13:3–4).

The New Empire Arising

With the terrorist attacks at the Brussels, Belgium, airport in March 2016 and at the Istanbul, Turkey, airport in July 2016, along with soft targets in France, the United States, Turkey, and other places, innocent men, women, and children were thrust into eternity. People are afraid and looking for a hero to end the violence. This "hero" will arise. He will at first appear nonviolent, promoting a global agenda of peace and security (2 Thess. 2:1–8). "He shall also set his face to enter with the strength of his whole kingdom, bringing with him a proposal of peace which he shall put into effect....He shall come in peaceably and obtain the kingdom by flatteries" (Dan. 11:17, 21).

This "hero" will be the Antichrist. He will offer peaceful solutions, and a new Europe will rapidly emerge out of the chaos, and I'm inclined to believe, based on Scripture, the new Europe will be the final world power (Dan. 2; 7).

Watch for more chaos in Europe and a powerful man calling for peace and security, and get ready for the "ride of your life" (1 Thess. 4:13–18). The prophetic signs are all in place, and it's time to draw closer to God than ever before, walk with Him, and be the ambassadors of Christ we were called to be on this earth.

> So we are ambassadors for Christ, as though God were pleading through us. We implore you in Christ's stead: Be reconciled to God.
> —2 Corinthians 5:20

Magog Nations

The prophet Ezekiel tells of a time when certain nations will attempt an invasion on Israel in the "latter days." This is one of the most interesting and important prophetic events because it is unprecedented. Such an alignment of nations has never happened in all of history until now.

> And the word of the Lord came to me, saying: Son of man, set your face against Gog of the land of Magog, the prince of Rosh, Meshek and Tubal, and prophesy against him, and say: Thus says the Lord God: I am against you, O Gog, the prince of Rosh, Meshek and Tubal. And I will turn you back and put hooks into your jaws, and I will bring you out, and all your army, horses, and horsemen, all of them clothed with all sorts of armor, even a great company with buckler and shield, all of them handling swords. Persia, Ethiopia, and Put with them, all of them with shield and helmet. I will do so to Gomer and all its troops, Beth Togarmah of the north quarters and all its troops, and many peoples with you.
> —Ezekiel 38:1–6

To identify this end-time coalition by the ancient names is challenging but not impossible. Prophecy "detectives" have done the research for us, and despite some disagreement over the precise locations of Meshek (Meshech in some translations) and Tubal, most scholars agree that the following is fairly accurate.

+ **Gog**—Gog is the leader of Magog and a very specific alliance of nations. Ezekiel sees Gog as the prince of Rosh, Meshek, and Tubal. Gog is most likely the political leader who puts together this Magog alliance in the last days.

+ **Magog**—There are many historical accounts of Russia being identified as Magog. We are told that in relation to Israel, Gog is coming from the far north regions. Russia is the farthest country directly north of Israel. The Jewish historian Josephus identified the land of Magog as Scythia, the progenitors of Russia to the north of Israel beyond the Black Sea.[10] This points to modern Russia.

+ **Prince of Rosh**—This is the leader of Magog, Meshek, and Tubal. The Hebrew identifies Rosh as "prince," "chief," or "leader." Some translations call him the "chief prince," or the leading man who organizes the coalition against Israel.

  Scholarly evidence has been presented that ancient Rosh is actually Russia today.[11] There is therefore little doubt that this prince of leaders, who organizes an invasion of Israel in the latter years, will be from the far north of Israel. If you draw a straight line north from Israel, you will go through Turkey and the Black Sea to find Moscow, the Russian capital lying directly to the far north of Jerusalem.

+ **Meshek and Tubal**—These nations, along with Magog, are the descendants of Japheth (Gen. 10:2), who settled in the far north regions beyond the Black Sea.[12] Some suggest that Meshek and Tubal are part of Turkey,[13] but they more likely are the Islamic countries in the southern part of the former Soviet Union. These include Azerbaijan (98.4 percent Muslim), Kazakhstan (56.4 percent Muslim), Kyrgyzstan (88.8 percent Muslim), Tajikistan (99 percent Muslim), Turkmenistan (93.3 percent Muslim), and Uzbekistan (96.5 percent Muslim).[14]

+ **Persia**—Persia (modern Iran), along with the other northern nations mentioned, will attack Israel in the latter days. Today Russia is supplying Iran with nuclear technology and assisting in the construction of nuclear power plants. Iran is also buying sophisticated antimissile and aircraft defense systems from Russia. Iran's stated reason is to protect itself from Israel's threats to destroy its nuclear ambitions.

+ **Ethiopia**—Modern Ethiopia has historically been a Christian nation but now is sandwiched directly between regions of ancient Ethiopia (Cush in some translations), which included Sudan to the north and west and Somalia to the south and east. Sudan and Somalia are both united in their hatred for Israel and have hosted terrorist networks like Al-Qaeda.[15] Sudan is armed with Iranian missiles for potential use against Israel.[16] Somalia is home to the terrorist network Al-Shabaab, known for its murderous attacks at malls and colleges.[17] Because Israel has been a reliable supplier of military assistance to modern Ethiopia and the two countries have enjoyed a good relationship,[18]

I personally do not believe that modern Ethiopia will take part in the Magog invasion of Ezekiel 38.

+ **Put**—Put is translated as Libya in many translations. Libya, another ally of Russia, is yet another Islamic nation with a history of being a forceful adversary of Israel.[19]

+ **Gomer**—A descendent of Japheth (Gen. 10:2), Gomer is part of the alliance against Israel in the latter days. Some scholars believe the name *Germany* came from the term *Gomerland*.[20] Other scholars believe ancient Gomer includes a larger portion of Eastern Europe and possibly regions of modern Turkey.[21]

+ **Togarmah**—This country encompasses regions of modern Turkey.[22] Turkey and Russia will align for this "Magog campaign." Led by its president, Recep Tayyip Erdoğan, a colorful, sporty, magnetic, and motivating Muslim leader, Turkey is experiencing a national fervor to return to the glory days of the Islamic Ottoman Empire.[23]

Reason for this Magog invasion

The invasion by this alliance could be a punitive action against Israel for its part in destroying many Islamic terrorists (Ps. 83), leveling Damascus in Syria (Isa. 17), and perhaps involvement in the massive devastation that is yet to come to southwestern Iran (Jer. 49). We don't yet know what the exact reason will be, but Russia has threatened in the past to attack Israel in response to its war with Syria,[24] and Russia's motivation will be "to take spoil" (Ezek. 38:12–13). While the Islamic nations involved want to annihilate Israel as their blood enemy, Russia sees only the booty—silver and gold, oil and natural gas.

When will this invasion take place?

Some commentators believe it will happen before the Tribulation. Some believe it will come toward the end of the Tribulation. Others suggest it will not happen until the end of the millennial kingdom age. Orthodox Jewish scholars teach that this battle will occur right before the construction of the third temple (Ezek. 40) and the coming of the Messiah.[25]

It's interesting to see how Ezekiel presents this vision chronologically:

+ Chapter 36—The promise of Israel's restoration in the last days

+ Chapter 37—The coming together of Israel again in the last days

+ Chapter 38—The Magog allies' attempt to invade Israel in the latter years

+ Chapter 39—The great failure of this invasion and the cleanup process

+ Chapter 40—The new temple built in Jerusalem

I lean toward the Orthodox Jewish view. I believe this Magog invasion will occur up to three and a half years before the beginning of the final *shabua*. It may occur before or after the Rapture of the church. Remember, the catching away of God's people in the Rapture is an event without any specific preview signs. But as we see the signs of the coming Tribulation, we know we are that much closer to our deliverance and resurrection.

The Spectator Nations That Question the Invasion

Sheba and Dedan

Remember the queen of Sheba who came to Israel to meet with King Solomon? (See 1 Kings 10.) Sheba was an Arabic nation, as was Dedan. This is proof that Arabs and Israelis can have a peaceful and cordial relationship. Ancient Sheba and Dedan were located in what is Saudi Arabia today.[26] Saudi Arabia will object to the Russian invasion, perhaps through the United Nations.

Tarshish

Tarshish was one of the sons of Javan (Gen. 10:4), who is known as the father of the Greek nation.[27] Jonah fled to Tarshish (Jon. 1:3), a distant land from Israel, probably located along the Mediterranean coast. It may be anywhere from modern Greece to modern Spain.[28] Other well-respected historians and scholars present compelling evidence that Tarshish once sat where Great Britain is today.[29]

Villages of Tarshish

These nations question and perhaps criticize Gog but do nothing (Ezek. 38:13). They, along with Saudi Arabia and Western Europe, are passive spectators in this Magog event. *Villages* in this passage is sometimes translated as "young lions" and may refer to nations colonized by people from Tarshish. If this is so, then America would be included, having originated from Europe. Some Bible prophecy teachers believe that the United States *could* be a village of Tarshish, which we will discuss in the next chapter. If the United States is included, we find it is either greatly weakened by that time or simply has no will to do anything except criticize. Even though these "village" nations question and denounce the invasion, their concern seems to have no moral focus, only material interests about plunder, booty, silver, and gold (Ezek. 38:13).

Let's recap who is involved in this coming invasion: Magog (Russia), Meshek and Tubal (probably southern former Soviet states), Persia (Iran), Ethiopia (Sudan and Somalia but most likely not modern Ethiopia), Put (Libya), Gomer (Germany or Eastern Europe), and Togarmah (Turkey).

Unfortunately for Russia and her Islamic allies, the invasion goes terribly wrong. God intervenes, and most of the invading military forces are destroyed by a series of unusual events. As armies sneak into the mountains of Israel to prepare their surprise attack, an earthquake kills many and brings such confusion to the invading forces that they begin to kill each other (Ezek. 38:19–21). If that weren't enough, the arrows (missiles) they bring begin to detonate in their hands (Ezek. 39:3). The picture God paints is one of nuclear, chemical, and biological weapons backfiring on the invaders, killing five-sixths of the invading horde (Ezek. 38:19–39:6, kjv).

It will be so devastating that it will take seven full months to find and bury all the dead (Ezek. 39:12). This will greatly cripple Russia's aggressive dreams and practically decimate Islamic military forces, and they will likely never recover. You can read the full account in Ezekiel 38–39. God will show that He is a covenant-keeping God, and the nations of the world will know that God's hand defended Israel: "Thus I will magnify Myself, and sanctify Myself, and I will be known in the eyes of many nations. Then they shall know that I am the Lord" (Ezek. 38:23).

Terrorist Groups

At first glance Psalm 83 appears to be another imprecatory prayer against Israel's enemies. But a closer look may show ISIS and other terrorist organizations in a prophetic light. If this is not merely a prayer but a prophetic forecast, terrorist groups around Israel should be very afraid.

We see a totally different coalition in Psalm 83 than we see in Ezekiel 38–39. Researcher and author Bill Salus is, in my opinion, one of the most devoted and brilliant prophecy researchers of our day. Bill studied this psalm for over a decade, poring over volumes of research material. Bill provided me with invaluable guidance in this section.[30]

Let me explain. Asaph, the writer of this psalm, was more than a psalmist. He was recognized as a prophet and seer in Israel (1 Chron. 25:1–2; 2 Chron. 29:30). Asaph served the Lord and His people as a singing prophet, recorder, leader, songwriter, and prophetic intercessor. The account of all that Asaph achieved is quite remarkable.

As a reliable and credible prophet, Asaph may have been prophesying a future event while writing Psalm 83. The most interesting part of this psalm is that he describes an alignment of groups, located in specific regions, that has never occurred in the past. Asaph lists, almost like a secret intelligence report, groups aligning against Israel and carefully specifies where they will be located by providing the ancient geographical locations. But first he describes their attitudes toward Israel:

> Your enemies make an uproar, and those who hate You have lifted up their heads. They have given crafty counsel against Your people, and have consulted against Your treasured ones. They have said, "Come, and let us cut them off from being a nation, that the name of Israel may be no more remembered." For they have conspired together; they make a covenant against You.
>
> —VERSES 2–5

So the groups Asaph talks about in Psalm 83 hate the living God (v. 2); consult against God's treasured people, the Jews (v. 3); deny Israel's right to exist as a nation and are determined to cut off Israel from being a nation (v. 4); and conspire together and make a covenant against the true and living God (v. 5).[31]

Beginning in verse 6, Asaph describes the exact locations of these prophetic groups:

> The tabernacles of Edom, and the Ishmaelites; of Moab, and the Hagarenes; Gebal, and Ammon, and Amalek; the Philistines with the inhabitants of Tyre; Assur also is joined with them: they have holpen the children of Lot. Selah.
>
> —VERSES 6–8, KJV

Let's identify these groups and where they are positioned geographically today, remembering that the prophets of old, when speaking of last days' events, used the regional names of their day to identify their future localities.[32]

- ✦ **Edom**—*Edom* means the descendants of Esau. Some modern-day Palestinians are descended from the Edomites.[33] Although not all Palestinians have descended from the Edomites, Esau has definite

ethnical representation within the Palestinian people
of today.

+ **Ishmaelites**—*Ishmaelites* refers to all Arabs.

+ **Moab**—Moab today is central Jordan, and some
Palestinians are descendants of Moabites.

+ **Hagarenes**—The Hagarenes are Egyptians, perhaps
referring to the Muslim Brotherhood, founded in
Egypt.

+ **Gebal**—Gebal is located in Lebanon, home of the ter-
rorist group Hezbollah. Other radical terrorist and
jihadist groups operating in Lebanon include Hamas,
Palestinian Islamic Jihad, Popular Front for the
Liberation of Palestine, Abu Nidal Organization, al-
Jihad, Asbat al-Ansar, Fatah al-Islam, and others.[34]

+ **Ammon**—*Ammon* refers to northern Jordan, where
some Palestinian refugees reside. Today Jordan is
home to the terrorist group Takfiri-Salafi.[35]

+ **Amalek**—*Amalek* refers to Arabs to the south of
Israel. To the south and west of Israel, terrorist organizations associated with Al-Qaeda are growing,
including in the Gaza Strip and the Sinai Peninsula.[36]

+ **Philistines**—The Philistines are those residing in
today's Gaza Strip, including Palestinian refugees
and Hamas. When the Romans destroyed the Jewish
state, they sought to erase all memories of the Jewish
people's connection with their homeland. Thus, Rome
renamed the land Palestinia (Palestine) to honor
Israel's enemies, the Philistines.[37]

+ **Tyre**—Tyre is southern Lebanon, home of the terrorist group Hezbollah.

+ **Assur**—Assur (ancient Assyria) includes Syria and perhaps Northern Iraq, the current locations of ISIS terrorist networks.

+ **Children of Lot**—The children of Lot are Palestinians.[38]

In an amazing fashion, Asaph precisely described the geographical locations of the modern terrorist organizations surrounding Israel today. This includes the Muslim Brotherhood of Egypt, Hamas, Hezbollah, Palestinian terrorism groups, and ISIS. Notice that Iran is not included in this Psalm 83 list. While Iran has supported other terrorist groups, ISIS is a thorn in Iran's flesh.[39] ISIS is Sunni Muslim and Iran is predominantly Shiite Muslim. Iran has designs on controlling the entire Middle East, but ISIS has thrown a wrench into Iran's plans.[40]

If I am correct in understanding Asaph's exact groupings of these terrorist locations, then it is certain the rest of his prophetic intercession regarding their destruction shall be fulfilled also (Ps. 83:9–18).

Terrorists Terrorized and Neutralized

The demise of these groups may come at the hand of the Israeli Defense Forces (possibly with assistance from the United States), or God may intervene supernaturally, but one thing is certain: the terrorists around Israel are going to be terrorized and neutralized themselves. This will be a dramatic humiliation for the Islamic jihadists.

My personal belief is that this shocking event will occur *before* the Magog invasion of Ezekiel 38–39. Some of my colleagues believe Psalm 83 describes part of the Magog invasion, but the participants in the two events are all different from the other. The stage is now being set. It will be interesting to watch as these amazing prophecies come to pass.

Syria

A few years ago I was conducting a prophecy seminar at a large church in the Midwest. After one of the sessions, we had time for questions. One fellow came to the microphone and asked what I believed about the Damascus prophecy in Isaiah 17 and the Psalm 83 prophecy. Though I had been studying Bible prophecy for more than forty years, I didn't know the answer.

I started researching and concluded that these prophecies have not been completely fulfilled. The Isaiah 17 prophecy is: "Damascus will cease from being a city; it shall be a ruinous heap" (v. 1).

Damascus had a population of about 1.7 million as of 2009.[41] The city has mosques, churches, and cultural centers. Damascus is also the seat of Syria's government, where the regime of President Bashar al-Assad is located.

Syria has insistently demanded that Israel give back the Golan Heights, threatening missile attacks if Israel fails to comply.[42] The discovery of oil reserves in the Golan Heights area has made it even more attractive.[43] But Prime Minister Netanyahu minced no words in responding, warning that Israel will respond fiercely if Syria attempts to attack.[44]

Syrian rebels rose against President al-Assad in 2011, provoking a civil war. But the civil war created something far worse than Bashar al-Assad's regime—the savage ISIS took advantage of the crisis and began implementing its jihadist brand of Islam. Similarly, when American troops were prematurely removed from Iraq, ISIS seized the opportunity and ravaged much of Iraq. Christian men were beheaded and their wives and daughters taken into slavery. The cruelty of this group of terrorists is beyond anything most of us have seen.

Al-Assad may feel like he needs to do something dramatic to save his country and his throne, but the Israeli Defense Forces will "respond in strength" to any Syrian attempts to harm their country.[45] The world will condemn Israel, but what difference does it make? It seems the nations are systematically turning their backs on Israel, the precious apple of God's eye.

Watch Syria and pray for the Syrian people caught in the crossfire of history.

Elam

Another prophecy that has never been fully fulfilled concerns Elam, located in southwestern Iran. This prophecy may be fulfilled simultaneously with the Ezekiel 38–39 prophecy when Iran unites with Russia in a failed invasion, but it quite possibly may occur prior to the Magog invasion.

Modern-day Iran is comprised of ancient Elam and Persia. One of the most "strategic and vulnerable nuclear targets" in Iran is the Bushehr nuclear reactor, located in ancient Elam. A nuclear accident here would rival the Chernobyl nuclear disaster of 1986.[46] We know Iran is enriching uranium today for its nuclear aspirations.

In the Book of Jeremiah, we read, "For I will cause Elam to be dismayed before their enemies, and before those who seek their life. And I will bring disaster upon them, even My fierce anger, says the Lord; and I will send the sword after them until I have consumed them" (49:37). The devastation in Elam will produce a monstrous refugee crisis. Christian relief organizations must be prepared, because God said He is coming to Elam with His authority (throne) to gather people who turn to Christ and restore their fortunes in the latter days (Jer. 49:38–39).

If you would like to study this further from a master researcher, I recommend the book *Nuclear Showdown in Iran: Revealing the Ancient Prophecy of Elam* by Bill Salus.[47]

Islam Is Approaching Its Demise

Present world conditions show us that the stage is being set for a grand finale. It's clear to me that Islam is about to take some serious losses. It will be greatly weakened as we approach the Day of the Lord.

Here are six specific reasons I believe Islam will diminish and become severely crippled as we approach the coming of Christ:

1. Because of the prophecies of devastation against Elam—Elam is located in the southwest portion of modern Iran and is the site of the Bushehr nuclear reactor (Jer. 49)

2. Because of Syrian losses in the destruction of Damascus (Isa. 17)

3. Because of the shattering of Muslim terrorist organizations (Ps. 83)

4. Because of the severe Islamic losses from the invasion foretold in Ezekiel 38–39

5. Because of the coming Euphrates River disaster foretold in Revelation, in which tens of millions will die— four predominantly Islamic nations are affected by the Euphrates River: Turkey, Syria, Iraq, and to a lesser degree, Iran (Rev. 9:14; 16:12)

6. Because Islam is totally incompatible with the religion of the prophesied coming world leader (2 Thess. 2:4)

In spite of what is coming to Islamic nations, God loves the Arab people. He could have let their patriarch, Ishmael, die as a young boy. Instead, God promised to make him a great nation and to bless him (Gen. 17:20). After all, Abraham was the father of both Ishmael and Isaac. But the religion of Islam has blinded many Arabic people to the amazing love of Father God. Islam teaches that God can have no son, thus they firmly believe that Jesus cannot be God's Son, preventing them from receiving the full benefits as children of Abraham.

That is changing. Unprecedented numbers of Muslims are coming to Jesus Christ in Saudi Arabia, Iran, and Syria, along with great numbers among the refugees fleeing from ISIS. Evangelists are reporting historic numbers of Muslims are turning to Jesus, some at a great cost.[48] Dreams, visions, and miracles are being reported among Muslims, leading them to faith in Jesus.[49]

We must pray for Muslims to have supernatural experiences that will lead them to the truth of the gospel while we stand with Israel for its salvation as well.

> Look among the nations, and watch—wonder and be amazed! For I am doing a work in your days that you would not believe, though it were told you.
>
> —Habakkuk 1:5

China

Napoleon once said, "China is a sleeping giant. Let her sleep, for when she wakes she will move the world." [50] China is already being called the world's next superpower. [51] Bible commentators often tie Revelation 9:17–19 with Revelation 16:12 and suggest that both passages refer to China. But I'm not so sure these prophecies should be tied together.

> The sixth angel poured out his bowl on the great Euphrates River, and its water was dried up, to prepare the way for the kings from the East.
>
> —Revelation 16:12

If the prophecies in Revelation 9 and 16 are referring to the same army, there are only three possibilities as to who the kings from the East could represent. We are told the number of the army will be two hundred million (Rev. 9:16). Only three groups would have the fighting capacity to reach that number.

1. China (This is what most prophecy scholars teach.)

2. India

3. The Muslim world east of Israel and the Euphrates (If Muslim nations or groups united, they could easily muster an army of two hundred million.)

India has not previously shown aggressive designs against Israel, so I would dismiss it as a candidate. In fact, India is the largest buyer of Israeli military equipment and is the third largest Asian trade partner of Israel.[52] India has consistently abstained from voting in resolutions against Israel in the United Nations.[53] That could change under a global government, but it's not likely.

What about the prospect of two hundred million Muslims crossing the Euphrates? That is not likely for a simple reason: prior to the time when the kings of the East cross the Euphrates, Islam will already be fairly decimated by the Ezekiel 38–39 Magog invasion, Psalm 83 devastation, Isaiah 17 losses, and Jeremiah 49 prophecies of desolation. Also, the Antichrist forces will have no use for Islam or any religion, so Islam will be neutralized by the Antichrist forces and natural disasters and supernatural calamities foretold by the prophets.

The only other option for kings of the East appears to be China. However, I believe the catastrophic crisis of Revelation 9 may be part of the failed invasion of Israel foretold by Ezekiel, and the event of Revelation 16 is entirely different.

The Euphrates forms a natural barrier against the armies of the Eastern world. The sixth bowl judgment of the apocalypse will dry up that river to make way for the kings of the East. Revelation 9:13–16 and 16:12 speak of two separate armies. The army in Revelation 9 may include large numbers from Middle Eastern nations that cross the Euphrates with catastrophic effect. Hundreds of millions of people shockingly die.

This particular army is obviously equipped with weapons of mass destruction (nuclear, chemical, or biological), and the situation occurs as the world is already in the final *shabua*. Revelation 9:13–16 could actually be describing part of the campaign of Ezekiel 38–39, the attempted Magog invasion of Israel. The armies of Iran (ancient Persia) are listed as active participants of the Magog invasion and quite possibly could cross the Euphrates to fulfill their assigned role in the combined invasion.

Here's another question that arises as we read this Euphrates prophecy in Revelation 9. Why would these armies be on horses instead of flying in planes, launching missiles, and moving heavy artillery? There are three possibilities.

1. John the Revelator saw primarily a picture of the demonic world. John is being shown something in the spirit realm. It involves releasing four angels that are bound at the Euphrates. He described the horses as having heads of lions with fire, smoke, and brimstone proceeding out of their mouths. However, there are no horses in the natural realm with heads of lions and mouths that emit fire, smoke, and brimstone, so it's possible that this is a spiritual vision of the demonic world. (See Revelation 9:13–19.)

2. John saw a natural army. Some commentators suggest that John's description of horses with heads of lions and mouths that emit fire, smoke, and brimstone is a description of modern weaponry, which could be the case. The soldiers could be riding horses instead of using tanks because of an EMP annihilating all electronics, forcing the battle to be fought without modern technology.

3. John saw a combination of both scenarios, spiritual and physical.

The Revelation 9 Euphrates event likely will occur early in the first forty-two months of the Tribulation, whereas the Revelation 16:12 crossing of the Euphrates will take place sometime in the last two months of the second half of the seven-year Tribulation. The Euphrates River formed the eastern boundary of the ancient Roman Empire, and the army from the East will cross this river in the coming world conflict known as Armageddon. We often think of Armageddon as one final war, but in reality there will be several stages to Armageddon, including the eventual involvement of China and perhaps North Korea and other nations east of the Euphrates.

Why will the armies from the East in Revelation 16 come to Israel during the final months of the Tribulation? They are not coming for spoil as in the Ezekiel 38–39 attempted invasion, which I suggest may be connected to the Euphrates incident in Revelation 9. The kings of the East in Revelation 16 are coming in response to demonic ambassadors who convince them that this last phase of the battle will put an end to the relentless judgments that have befallen the citizens of the world during the Tribulation (Rev. 16:13–14). In Satan's mind this will be his final attempt to prevent Christ's return. Again, this crossing of the Euphrates in Revelation 16 occurs near the end of the Tribulation.

We are the first generation to witness China reaching a place of potentially being able to fulfill the Revelation 16 prophecy. China represents almost 20 percent of the world's population and is the fourth largest nation by area. China may soon gain control of most of the countries of the East. China's Communist leadership is ruthlessly strategic and has built one of the most formidable militaries in the world today. China is not going away from the world scene and will be a principal player as we move toward Armageddon and the second coming of Christ.

It's stunning to watch how the nations of the world are strategically lining up precisely as we were shown by the biblical prophets of old. We have seen strategic realignments in our generation that eventually will lead to a one-world government and usher the world into the seven-year period known as the Tribulation.

But what about the United States?

Chapter 7

THE UNITED STATES IN BIBLE PROPHECY

WHAT THE FUTURE HOLDS FOR THIS SUPERPOWER

Blessed is the nation whose God is the LORD.
—PSALM 33:12

WHAT WILL HAPPEN to the United States in the days ahead? Are there biblical prophecies about America? Why does the United States seem absent in the pages of the Bible? How can it be that our country, once the wealthiest, most evangelistic, most generous, and most powerful nation in all of history, plays no discernible role in the dominant prophetic events of this age?

Other places, like Russia, parts of Asia, and parts of Europe are named by their historical regions, but the United States is not mentioned directly. Through the lens of Bible prophecy, the United States is conspicuously missing from the geopolitical scene. What happened? Where is America to be found in Bible prophecy? Can it be found? Let's run through some of the possibilities before arriving at what I think is the conclusion.

A Village of Tarshish?

Some of the best prophecy scholars teach that the United States is one of the villages of Tarshish listed in Ezekiel 38: "Sheba and Dedan and the merchants of Tarshish with all its villages shall say to you, 'Have you come to take spoil? Have you gathered your company to seize prey, to carry away silver and gold, to take away livestock and goods, to take great spoil?'" (v. 13).

Historians suggest that Tarshish was located in either Great Britain or Spain, and the United States by extension is one of her villages, or a younger nation that was colonized from these European countries. So the United States *may* be here in Ezekiel 38, but it apparently remains passive or unable to do anything when Russia aligns with the Muslim nations to invade Israel. In other words, when this war occurs, the United States could already be weakened to the point of being unable to do anything but stand on the sidelines.

The Eagle of Revelation 12?

Another theory, which requires a good deal of creative speculation and allegorizing, is that the United States is the eagle of Revelation 12:

> When the dragon saw that he was cast down to the earth,
> he persecuted the woman who gave birth to the male Child.
> The woman was given two wings of a great eagle, that she
> might fly into the wilderness to her place, where she is to
> be nourished for a time and times and half a time, from the
> presence of the serpent.
>   —REVELATION 12:13–14

Teachers of this concept point out that the eagle is a conspicuous symbol of the United States. The problem is that the eagle was also a symbol of the Roman Empire.[1] In fact, many nations have used the eagle as a national symbol, including Austria, Palestine, Russia, Syria, and at least twenty-five other countries.[2]

By letting the Bible interpret the Bible, we see exactly who the eagle is. Just as there is no doubt that the dragon in this passage represents Satan, there is little doubt that the eagle of Revelation 12 represents God Himself. God has always described His care for His people as that of an eagle (e.g., Exod. 19:4; Deut. 32:11–12).

The New Babylon?

Another frequently mentioned idea is that the United States is the prophetic Babylon seen in Revelation 17. I have heard some really well-prepared sermons about America being Babylon or Mystery Babylon. In recent years the United States has become like Babylon in many ways, spiritually and culturally. Nonetheless, we always need to go back to God's Word and read it very carefully. We need to understand Bible prophecy in its context and not by our own predisposition or cultural context.

In Revelation 17 we find "Mystery, Babylon the Great." John wrote:

> One of the seven angels who had the seven bowls came and talked with me, saying to me, "Come, I will show you the judgment of the great prostitute who sits on many waters, with whom the kings of the earth committed adultery, and the inhabitants of the earth were made drunk with the wine of her sexual immorality."...On her forehead a name was written: MYSTERY, BABYLON THE GREAT, THE MOTHER OF PROSTITUTES AND OF THE ABOMINATIONS OF THE EARTH.
>
> —Verses 1–2, 5

When we stick with the context, we discover that Mystery Babylon the Great represents a false, end-time religious system. The original Babylon laid the foundation for all false religion. Its primary feature was false religion and unity. An end-time, conglomerate, syncretistic religion will form the Mystery Babylon of Revelation 17.

Now let's look at the Babylon of Revelation 18. This will be the political and commercial seat of the Antichrist's government during the Tribulation. Some commentators believe the city will actually be rebuilt. They were very excited when Saddam Hussein, former leader of Iraq, was planning to rebuild the city of Babylon. Because prophetic Babylon is a specific city, not a nation, it cannot be the United States: "Alas, alas for that great city, that mighty city, Babylon!" (Rev. 18:10).

In Revelation we read concerning the fall of Babylon:

"Fallen! Fallen is Babylon the Great!" She has become a dwelling place of demons, a haunt for every unclean spirit, and a haunt for every unclean and hateful bird. For all the nations have drunk of the wine of the wrath of her sexual immorality, the kings of the earth have committed adultery with her, and the merchants of the earth have become rich through the abundance of her luxury.

—Verses 18:1–3

I have heard some compelling arguments that Babylon is actually New York City. It's quite possible that in New York we are seeing preview signs of what is to come, making the city much like ancient Babylon. We witnessed the image of the demon goddess Kali projected on the Empire State Building,[3] along with the degradation of the rainbow, the symbol of God's covenant of mercy in judgment (Gen. 9:13–16) and authority (there is a rainbow around His throne in Revelation 4:3), when the rainbow colors lit up the Freedom Tower in New York to celebrate same-sex marriage.[4] In September 2016 a replica of the pagan arch that served as the entrance to the temple of Ba'al in ancient days was unveiled in New York. Rabbi Jonathan Cahn was there to warn America of the sobering implications.[5]

It is true there is power in imagery. Artifacts, images, and idols can actually become spiritual portals between the physical world and the unseen world of the demonic. I know that sounds strange, but those who have studied this dimension of the demonic agree that Satan loves setting up physical indicators of his presence, whether it's through wicked images or by seizing and corrupting a symbol belonging to God.

Nevertheless, I personally do not believe New York City or the United States is the Babylon or Mystery Babylon of Bible prophecy. There is no scriptural evidence for it, and it seems an arbitrary position, though again, the wickedness that takes place in New York City is a preview sign of what prophetic Babylon will be like. Most scholars and students of Bible prophecy, including me, understand Mystery Babylon to be a syncretistic conglomeration of religions that forms in the last days. This religious juggernaut will be instrumental in supporting the coming world leader's policies. Literal Babylon may be rebuilt, but the Babylon named in Revelation 18 is most likely a symbolic term for the coming world empire's capital city and headquarters of the final world leader, the Antichrist.

Sudden and Dramatic Decline

If the United States is not Babylon or any of the other possibilities above, where is it in Bible prophecy? I agree with Britt Gillette, who says, "It's likely that America's fall from power will be sudden and dramatic."[6] The prophetic silence concerning America seems to show us that power will shift away from the United States—meaning America has no major role in Bible prophecy whatsoever. That means the future of our country will not look like our past—and that things may change suddenly.

I grew up in the 1950s and 1960s. Our mailman carried a bag of mail through the neighborhood and often stopped for a glass of lemonade and a pleasant chat. There was a seasonal root beer stand near our home, and we were always excited when the owner returned from the South to open our favorite hangout. The owner of the gas station on the corner often gave people credit when they couldn't afford a tank of gas. When I was fifteen, the gas station owner gave me my first real job.

Neighbors did things together back then—picnics, get-togethers, and even vacations. If we left home for a few days to visit relatives and forgot to lock our doors, we knew it would be OK because neighbors watched out for one another.

Every Sunday cars pulled out of driveways in almost every home in the neighborhood, heading for church. Some attended the Methodist church, others the Baptist church, and others the Catholic church. My family, after the obligatory complaining from my brother and me, would hop in the big Buick and head downtown to Trinity Lutheran Church. We all knew the Lord's Prayer, the Apostles' Creed, and

John 3:16. I can't say that everyone was a committed Christian, but we respected God and each other. Life seemed good.

I don't recall any drug use in all my school years. Sure, we would try to get our hands on some beer or wine, but that was the worst of it. When a man tried to show an "adult movie" in downtown Jackson, Michigan, he was immediately arrested on obscenity charges.

We still had our challenges, family arguments, hormonal fits, teen rebellion, and so on, but it was mild compared to the challenges young people face today. Teachers cared about their students, and we knew the police officers and even the city bus drivers by name. We were a community.

Somehow America changed. There were landmarks along the way. The *Abington School District v. Schempp* and *Murray v. Curlett* lawsuits led to a Supreme Court ruling ending official Bible reading in American public schools in 1963.

Within a few years the drug revolution exploded. "Free sex" became a way of life, and with it came the dramatic rise of sexually transmitted diseases. Self-proclaimed messiahs like mass-murderer Charles Manson rose up to deceive. Popular music lyrics changed from sporty cars and puppy love to enchanting drugs, Satan, suicide, and violence.

A decade after Bible reading and prayer in public schools were abolished, the *Roe v. Wade* Supreme Court decision opened the floodgates to the slaughter of innocent babies—nearly sixty million since 1973.[7] In Exodus 21:22–25 the death penalty was issued for anyone who caused the death of a baby in his or her mother's womb. It's clear from Scripture that God considers a baby in the womb to be just as much a human being as a living adult. Abortion is not about a woman's right to choose. It is a matter of choosing the death of a helpless human being made in God's image (Gen. 1:26–27; 9:6). But America began sacrificing its children on the altar of convenience.

Television programming that once taught moral lessons faded, and television became a primary venue for the display and promotion of immoral lifestyles. The prophet Isaiah warned us, "Woe to those who call evil good, and good evil; who exchange darkness for light, and light for darkness; who exchange bitter for sweet, and sweet for bitter!" (Isa. 5:20).

The United States was blessed and protected by God but chose a path of moral decay. We are now in a state of moral rot beyond anything we would have imagined just a few years ago. "In God we trust," "one nation under God," and "all men are created equal" (with an emphasis on *created*) have gone away. Benjamin Rush, who signed the Declaration of Independence and ratified the US Constitution, wrote, "The gospel of Jesus Christ prescribes the wisest rules for just conduct in every situation of life. Happy are they who are enabled to obey them in all situations!"[8]

The biggest tragedy has been that many pulpits in America are silent about what is happening to our nation. "Don't judge," the pastors say. "Don't talk about sin or hell. Don't make people uncomfortable." Those are the rules of the day for many preachers. Yet the church possesses the only hope for our nation. People don't appreciate the light until the darkness, sin, and bondage are exposed and explained (Rom. 6:23; Eph. 5:11).

In Matthew 24 and Luke 17 Jesus promised to return in a time like that of Noah and Lot. Their cultures approved of moral depravity, violence, and betrayal. Interestingly, to the citizens back then, it seemed like "business as usual" until it was too late to get on the boat, too late to run from Sodom. Their lives were over, and now eternity stared them in the face. As Solomon wrote, "Righteousness exalts a nation, but sin is a reproach to any people" (Prov. 14:34).

America Has Been Warned

Moses issued a solemn warning to the children of Israel, explaining the blessings of obeying God and the national curses of disobedience (Deut. 28–29). Those words now echo from shore to shore over America, as if Moses were speaking directly to us. If the people of Israel (or any other nation) heeded his timeless words, they would receive the following blessings:

+ God would set their nation high above all others (28:1).

+ God would overtake them with all kinds of blessings (28:2).

+ Their children would be blessed and fruitful (28:4).

+ They would be productive and experience increase (28:4).

+ The Lord would cause all their enemies to be defeated (28:7).

+ Everything they set their hand to would be blessed (28:8).

+ The Lord would cause them to overflow in prosperity (28:11).

+ The Lord would ensure cooperative weather patterns (28:12).

+ They would not need to borrow but would have the means to lend to other nations (28:12).

+ The Lord would make them the head and not the tail, always above and not beneath (28:13).

Moses continued, "But it will happen, if you will not listen to the voice of the Lord your God, by being careful to do all His commandments and His statutes which I am commanding you today, that all these curses will come upon you and overtake you" (Deut. 28:15). The "curse pattern" Moses lays out is predictable and clearly spelled out. When a nation ignores and offends God and does not turn back to Him, the following things happen:

+ A general curse will arrive over the land (28:15–17).

+ Their children and real estate will come under a curse (28:18–19).

+ Perplexing problem after problem will visit the nation, from financial to medical problems (28:20–22, 27).

+ Economic problems will go from bad to worse, exacerbated by declining national productivity (28:23–24).

+ Military weakness will ensue, and the nation will no longer win (28:25–26).

+ Massive confusion will strike, with blindness and bewilderment (28:28).

+ Oppression and continual losses will come (28:29).

+ National productivity will decrease to deeper levels than ever (28:30–31, 38).

+ Dreams of a good life will be forever shattered (28:30–31).

+ The nation's children will be lost to another people (28:32).

+ Another nation will oppress, rob, and crush them, and the people will be helpless to do anything about it; all they have worked for will go to someone else (28:33).

+ The cursed nation will become an international object of ridicule instead of a respected world leader (28:37).

+ Their children will go into captivity, including possible addictions and rebellion (28:41).

+ Foreigners who have infiltrated the land will get the upper hand and become a higher priority; they will become the head, and the cursed people will become the tail; the cursed nation will need to borrow from foreigners (28:43–44).

+ The government will be taken over by fierce, harsh people who do not respect the old or show favor to

the young; the cursed people will be in dread day and
night and will have no assurance of life (28:49–50, 66).

Today aggressor nations and terrorist regimes no longer fear US
retaliation. Former vice president Dick Cheney said in 2012, "Our
allies no longer trust us, or have confidence in us and our adver-
saries no longer fear us." He went on to describe how the Middle
East has been moving in a direction "fundamentally hostile to the
long term US interest" and how the US "is unable to influence events
in that part of the world."[9] During the presidential election of 2016,
Donald Trump repeatedly warned that the United States military is
"depleted" and a "disaster."[10] Many agree with him that the US military is in worse condition than most realize.[11]

The United States is now the top debtor nation in the world. Today
the national debt is soaring to over $20 trillion. The interest expense
on the national debt in 2016 was $432,649,652,901.12.[12] The national
debt is nearing "terminal velocity," a point at which default may be
necessary.[13] Thousands of US jobs and hundreds of companies have
been exported to other countries.[14]

The harbingers have arrived in America. But if we will turn back to
God, trusting Him to help us take serious action toward correcting
the missteps of our past, I believe He will bring a restorative miracle
to this nation. Otherwise America may become too weak to take any
action to protect its citizens against hostile aggressors.

> You did not serve the LORD your God with joy and with
> gladness of heart, for the abundance of all things. Therefore,
> you will serve your enemies.
>
> —DEUTERONOMY 28:47–48

Two Pillars of the United States

The first president of the United States, George Washington, gave
a sobering warning, just as Moses did, in his farewell address on
September 19, 1796. He emphasized the two "great Pillars of human
happiness," which he identified as "Religion and morality," and

reminded his listeners that these are the "firmest props of the duties of men and citizens." He stated, "Of all the dispositions and habits which lead to political prosperity, Religion and morality are indispensable supports." He capitalized the word "Religion," referring to Christianity.[15]

Washington sounded like Paul, speaking to his beloved flock before leaving them:

> Therefore take heed to yourselves and to the entire flock, over which the Holy Spirit has made you overseers, to shepherd the church of God which He purchased with His own blood. For I know that after my departure, dreadful wolves will enter among you, not sparing the flock. Even from among you men will arise speaking perverse things, to draw the disciples away after them. Therefore watch, remembering that for three years night and day I did not cease to warn everyone with tears.
>
> —ACTS 20:28–31

In recent years the United States has crossed boundaries that brought the demise of other nations. We will never be able to say the prophets did not warn us. I recently heard Messianic Jewish rabbi Jonathan Cahn, author of *The Harbinger* and *The Mystery of the Shemitah*, say on a radio program, "America is now overripe for God's judgment." Rabbi Cahn continued, "If you're not born again, you must be born again, and this is the time....If you are a believer...if there's anything in our life that is not right, we need to get it out now."[16]

A person or nation that does not turn away from wickedness can go too far and too long, and then it becomes too late. Jeremiah warned Israel over and over again, but they mocked and ridiculed him. He tried interceding for them, but God said it was too late. Israel would go into captivity in Babylon for seventy years as a result of their repeated disobedience.

> As for you, do not pray for this people, nor lift up a cry nor prayer for them, nor make intercession to Me, for I will not

hear you. Do you not see what they do in the cities of Judah
and in the streets of Jerusalem?

—Jeremiah 7:16–17

We find this exact theme in the New Testament in Paul's letter to
the Romans. There is a point of no return when God turns people
over to a reprobate mind, lost without hope:

> And since they did not see fit to acknowledge God, God
> gave them over to a debased mind, to do those things which
> are not proper. They were filled with all unrighteousness,
> sexual immorality, wickedness, covetousness, malicious-
> ness; full of envy, murder, strife, deceit. They are gossips,
> slanderers, God-haters, insolent, proud, boastful, inven-
> tors of evil things, and disobedient toward parents, without
> understanding, covenant breakers, without natural affec-
> tion, calloused, and unmerciful, who know the righteous
> requirement of God, that those who commit such things are
> worthy of death. They not only do them, but also give hearty
> approval to those who practice them.
>
> —Romans 1:28–32

The Roman Empire experienced a decline and fall, and America is
following an eerily parallel path. Witnessing firsthand the deteriora-
tion of an empire is chilling. Rome went from a state of wealth and
influence into nonexistence, with many of the mile markers we have
already passed. America's decline may take generations as Rome's
did. The United States may one day become a satellite nation of the
New Europe. Depending on its decisions and actions toward God in
the days ahead, America's demise may come suddenly due to nuclear
attack, EMP attack, financial collapse, or foreign invasion.

But there is a much better possibility and conceivably an extrava-
gantly brighter future than this.

A Better Possibility

Prophecy isn't meant to frighten us; it is meant to enlighten us and give us hope. No matter how dark it gets, Jesus promises never to leave us or forsake us but to walk with us and work with us (Matt. 28:20; Heb. 13:5). As the darkness deepens, the light of Christ in us will grow brighter.

> We should live soberly, righteously, and in godliness in this present world, as we await the blessed hope and the appearing of the glory of our great God and Savior Jesus Christ, who gave Himself for us, that He might redeem us from all lawlessness and purify for Himself a special people, zealous of good works.
>
> —Titus 2:12–14

God never intended for us to walk in hopelessness. He intended for us to be people of faith, and faith is the substance of things we hope for (Heb. 11:1). God is calling us as ambassadors of Christ to be hope distributors in these last days (2 Cor. 5:20). Yes, America may collapse. But there is another possibility, a real hope—revival!

We have biblical precedent for this. If people listen and turn around, judgment can be softened or even averted, as it was for Nineveh.

> Jonah began to enter the city, going a day's walk. And he cried out, "In forty days' time, Nineveh will be overthrown!" So the people of Nineveh believed God, and proclaimed a fast. And everyone, great and small, put on sackcloth.... When God saw their actions, that they turned from their evil ways, He changed His mind about the disaster that He had said He would bring upon them, and He did not do it.
>
> —Jonah 3:4–5, 10

I believe strongly that we, as the church, are on the threshold of a whole new dimension of God's grace and glory. I believe we will be a twenty-first-century church with first-century power; we were handpicked by God to live in these times; an unleashing of God's glory, an anointing that past generations have prayed and fasted for, is coming; and God is preparing us for a greater level of testimony than the majority of people of all generations have ever heard about.

Now is the perfect time to intensify our fasting and prayer for America and its leaders. Every time people humbled themselves in fasting and prayer, without exception, God did something extraordinary. Even wicked King Ahab, a man sold out to the devil at a deep level, averted judgment when he humbled himself with fasting.

> When Ahab heard those words, he tore his clothes and put on sackcloth on his flesh and fasted and lay in sackcloth and walked meekly.
>
> The word of the Lord came to Elijah the Tishbite, saying, "See how Ahab humbles himself before Me? Because he humbles himself before Me, I will not bring the disaster during his lifetime, but during his son's lifetime I will bring the disaster on his household."
>
> —1 Kings 21:27–29

If believers will take their positions as His ambassadors on earth with the help of the Holy Spirit, God will heal this land, and we will win millions to Jesus Christ before His coming. Even so, come quickly, Jesus!

Chapter 8

THE MYSTERY NATION

YOU CARRY THE POWER OF ANOTHER WORLD

But you are a chosen race, a royal priesthood, a holy
nation, a people for God's own possession, so that
you may declare the goodness of Him who has called
you out of darkness into His marvelous light.
—1 PETER 2:9

THE BIBLE TELLS us about one more nation that is a critical player
in the end times. It's not Russia, Syria, China, Indonesia, or a
European or Latin American country. This nation is referred to as a
"mystery" nation, and it has a very diverse citizenry.

Mysteries are a big thing with God. He keeps mysteries throughout
history to be revealed at the right time. A mystery is simply a hidden
truth. The Greek word is *musterion*, a hidden or secret thing that
is not obvious to the understanding and sometimes defies understanding. (See 1 Corinthians 13:2; 14:2.) *Musterion* is derived from
muo, which means "to shut the mouth."[1]

Some of God's mysteries have unfolded already, and some are
yet future. For example, God kept some things hidden in ages past,
revealing them only after Christ's resurrection and ascension. They
are no longer mysteries because they became known. In the same way,
the mystery nation has become known at just the right time in history.

Mysteries in the Bible

The New Testament is filled with references to mysteries. Here are a few:

- Romans 11:25—the mystery of the Jews and Gentiles being saved through faith in Christ
- 1 Corinthians 2:7—the mystery of God's wisdom
- 1 Corinthians 15:51—the mystery of the Rapture
- Ephesians 1:9—the mystery of God's will
- Ephesians 3:1–3—the mystery of grace
- Ephesians 3:4 and Colossians 4:3—the mystery of Christ
- Ephesians 6:19—the mystery of the gospel
- Colossians 1:27—the mystery of Christ living in believers, the hope of glory
- Colossians 2:2 and Revelation 10:7—the mystery of God
- 2 Thessalonians 2:7—the mystery of lawlessness or iniquity
- 1 Timothy 3:9—the mystery of the faith
- Revelation 17:5—Mystery Babylon

Now we turn to the other mystery Jesus talked about, a mystery nation that would rise up and have a prominent role in the last days. He mentioned it to the Jewish leaders who rejected Him: "Therefore I tell you, the kingdom of God will be taken from you and given to a nation bearing its fruits" (Matt. 21:43).

The kingdom of God was going to be redirected from the ones to which it was offered and given to another nation that would be productive with its resources. The apostle Paul talked about this same mystery that God kept secret in ages past and revealed to the apostles and prophets of the New Testament:

> Now to Him who has power to establish you according to my gospel and the preaching of Jesus Christ, according to the revelation of the mystery, which was kept secret for long ages past.
>
> —ROMANS 16:25

> You may have heard…how by revelation He made known to me the mystery, as I have written briefly already, by which, when you read it, you may understand my knowledge of the mystery of Christ, which in other generations was not made known to the sons of men, as it is now revealed to His holy apostles and prophets by the Spirit.
>
> —EPHESIANS 3:2–5

This revelation was so astonishing that even the angels wished they were human so they could experience what the citizens of this new nation were experiencing—that is, God Himself living in them by His Spirit:

> It was revealed to them that they were not serving themselves but you, concerning the things which are now reported to you by those who have preached the gospel to you through the Holy Spirit, who was sent from heaven—things into which the angels desire to look.
>
> —1 PETER 1:12

This new nation, made up of Jews and Gentiles, men and women of all races and languages, would enjoy the presence of God working in and through their lives (John 1:11–12; Col. 1:27). As Peter put it, "But you are a chosen race, a royal priesthood, a holy nation, a people for God's own possession, so that you may declare the goodness of Him who has called you out of darkness into His marvelous light" (1 Pet. 2:9).

What is this mystery nation of which Jesus and the apostles prophesied? At one time I thought it was the United States, but I was wrong. This mystery nation is none other than the church of Jesus Christ. This nation without borders or earthly government will be the most important player in the end times.

When people become citizens of the church, this holy nation, seven distinct things occur:

1. They are transferred to a new kingdom (Col. 1:12–14).

2. The Spirit of God comes to live in them (2 Tim. 1:14).

3. They have all the promises of God available to them (2 Cor. 1:20).

4. They become kings and priests in the nation (Rev. 1:5–6).

5. They are given authority from the King to act as ambassadors (2 Cor. 5:20).

6. They are hope distributors for those who are not yet citizens of this mystery nation (Luke 9:2; Rom. 5:5–6).

7. They carry the power of another world everywhere they go (Luke 10:19; Acts 1:8).

Agents of Another World

The mystery nation represents another world—God's kingdom. Ultimately no nation on earth can defeat the mystery nation. Jesus said, "I will build My church, and the gates of Hades shall not prevail against it" (Matt. 16:18).

Many pastors and spiritual leaders seek to become powerful and influential on the earth by pursuing things like relevancy and political correctness. But these things don't make churches fruitful, effective, or vibrant. Neither do big buildings, awesome technology, great music, or a high educational level among the people. What sets the mystery nation apart is the presence of the King. Jesus said He would always be with us, even to the end of the age (Matt. 28:20). That means that everywhere you walk as a follower of Christ, you carry the power of another world. This may sound esoteric now, but this is the ultimate power that will rule the world. One day all human authority will bow to the King of this mystery nation, and we will rule with Him (Rev. 20:4, 6).

> Therefore God highly exalted Him and gave Him the name which is above every name, that at the name of Jesus every knee should bow, of those in heaven and on earth and under the earth, and every tongue should confess that Jesus Christ is Lord, to the glory of God the Father.
> —Philippians 2:9–11

For now our job is to give people hope that this mystery nation is open to all who come and will grow until the day our King literally rules the nations of the world. His presence, power, and love give people hope for now and eternity. The only legacy you will really leave is how much you became a hope distributor for this mystery nation before it is fully revealed.

The Lost in Need of Hope

If you ever visited our church in Lansing, I could introduce you to hundreds of people who once were considered hopeless and helpless until an ordinary member of the mystery nation introduced them to the real hope giver, Jesus.

I could introduce you to precious souls who once knew nothing but despair, rejection, and tragedy. You would meet former prostitutes who are now women of God; former alcoholics who are now sober and serving in the church; and ex-adulterers who are now faithful husbands. You would shake hands with people who were once bound by religion, now living free in Jesus—former Muslims, cult members, and others.

But this isn't unique to our church. These same testimonies are found in gospel-preaching churches all over the world, just as they were in the first century.

I remember an older fellow, once said to be a hopeless alcoholic. He was drinking a fifth of whiskey a day. When he visited our church at the persuasion of a member of the mystery nation, he realized there was hope for him. He ran to the altar as fast as he could to receive Jesus Christ as his Savior and Lord. When he did, he received real hope. From that time on, this man never had another drink of alcohol for the rest of his life. He loved to give his testimony about how he used to be nicknamed "Old Fifth-a-Day."

The citizens of that mystery nation are former drunks, ex-prostitutes, ex-whoremongers, ex-liars, ex-cheaters, and even former religionists, right along with those who grew up in church. Paul noticed the same kind of people joining the mystery nation in the first century:

> Do you not know that the unrighteous will not inherit the kingdom of God? Do not be deceived. Neither the sexually immoral, nor idolaters, nor adulterers, nor male prostitutes, nor homosexuals, nor thieves, nor covetous, nor drunkards, nor revilers, nor extortioners will inherit the kingdom of God. Such were some of you. But you were washed, you were sanctified, and you were justified in the name of the Lord Jesus by the Spirit of our God.
>
> —1 Corinthians 6:9–11

A Season of Revival

I have noticed in recent days a new outbreak of revival around the country. In West Virginia a youth evangelist began holding meetings at a local high school and church, and the Spirit of God drew thousands with a message of repentance and righteous living.[2] The mystery nation continues adding to its ranks.

At the Los Angeles Coliseum in April 2016, tens of thousands of people gathered for a remarkable all-day prayer and worship meeting. The sense of the presence of the King in that huge place was palpable, and many say it was the catalyst for a revival that may turn into the next great awakening our country needs.[3]

I have a question for you. Does hope tell people they are fine right where they are? Does the alcoholic need to hear that he is OK being an alcoholic? Does a homosexual need to hear that his lifestyle isn't really hurting him? No! Hope must clearly identify what is right and wrong, good and evil, so people understand their true condition. Ambassadors of the mystery nation must be bold in showing people their true condition and painting a picture of the radiant, hopeful future that is attainable through genuine faith.

We are watchmen on the wall, accountable to God to forewarn people of their true condition and offer them true hope. Ezekiel said it like this:

> Son of man, speak to the children of your people and say to them: If I bring a sword upon a land, and the people of the land take a man from among them and set him for their watchman, and he sees the sword come upon the land and blows the trumpet and warns the people, then whoever hears the sound of the trumpet and does not take warning, and a sword comes and takes him away, his blood shall be upon his own head. He heard the sound of the trumpet yet did not take warning. His blood shall be upon himself. But he who takes warning delivers his soul. But if the watchman sees the sword come and does not blow the trumpet and the people are not warned and a sword comes and takes a person from among them, he is taken away in his iniquity. But his blood I will require from the hand of the watchman.
>
> —EZEKIEL 33:2–6

As agents of God's kingdom we have the power and authority to bring the hope of rescue to those who are bound and hurting. We have the authority to offer each person we encounter a chance at a new life. *Hope* in the Greek language of the New Testament is "an expectation of good; a joyful and confident expectation of eternal salvation."[4] Hope is a blueprint for faith to operate effectively (Heb. 11:1–3). I like what Peter Kuzmic, missionary to Croatia, said: "Hope is the ability to hear the music of the future. Faith is the ability to dance to it in the present."[5]

Opening Blind Eyes

In the last days, hope will be one of earth's most precious commodities! If you have it, people will come to you seeking it like gold. They will want to know where you found it and how they can have some. The darker the world around us gets, the brighter our hope will shine. People will need hope more than they need food. As the Word says, "The spirit of a man will sustain his infirmity, but a wounded spirit who can bear?" (Prov. 18:14).

You carry the power of the Holy Spirit to open people's spiritually blind eyes to see the truth of their situation and to receive the hope of deliverance and salvation. Paul wrote that we have the authority to "open their eyes and to turn them from darkness to light, and from the power of Satan to God, that they may receive forgiveness of sins and an inheritance among those who are sanctified by faith" (Acts 26:18).

Jackie was legally blind from an aggressively advancing eye disease. She lived quite far from our church but heard that we believed in miracles, so she made the trek to Mount Hope Church. I called people forward for prayer during the service, and Jackie was among those who responded. Someone in our church, a normal, everyday hope distributor, laid hands on her as we prayed.

When the service was over, Jackie walked up to me and said softly, "Pastor, I was blind, but now I see." I did not know Jackie and thought she was having a spiritual experience. But she insisted, "No, Pastor, I came in here blind today, and now I can see perfectly." I asked her to go to her doctor for confirmation.

Later that week I received a handwritten letter from a doctor, who told me that Jackie had authorized him to write to me about her condition. He explained that she had an irreversible eye condition that would eventually leave her completely blind. He then told me that he examined her, and the condition was gone. The last line of his letter was this: "Pastor Williams, this is nothing short of a miracle." Jackie's healing started with hope and the obedience of a hope distributor from that mystery nation known as the church.

The apostle Peter described us as "a royal priesthood" (1 Pet. 2:9). Today we think of a priest as an ordained minister of a liturgical church with the authority to perform certain rites and administer certain sacraments. But biblical priests were those who stood in the gap between God and other people. Simply put, a priest is an intercessor. An intercessor prays for people and wars against the kingdom of darkness. Jesus is our great High Priest, and as His representatives, His ambassadors, we too are priests (Heb. 4:14–16; Rev. 1:6; 5:10).

Conflicting Prophecies?

Today we hear prophecies of a great revival and wonderful things ahead, but we also hear warnings of dark times on the horizon. How do we reconcile the two? Just as there are two sides of a coin, there are often two sides of prophecy: "Therefore consider the goodness and severity of God—severity toward those who fell, but goodness toward you" (Rom. 11:22).

In some cases the outcome, good or severe, depends on the mystery nation and its commitment to intercession. Prophecies, including those of impending judgment, are often conditional and can be limited or averted through repentance, humility, and intercession. The wicked city of Nineveh was forty days from annihilation, but the city fasted and prayed and God relented and postponed His judgment. God would much rather extend mercy than judgment.

Thank God for people like Lou Engle, Dutch Sheets, Dick Eastman, Mary Colbert, and other visionary prayer leaders who are raising up intercessors for our nation! Maybe the work of the mystery nation in our day can literally save America from its well-earned judgments.

In the Old Testament, 2 Chronicles 7:14 says that if God's people will take certain and specific actions, then God will send healing. Notice the *if*. God loves America and the American people. Nonetheless, God doesn't tolerate unrepentant sin and rebellion forever. We could be at a flash point now.

If My people, who are called by My name, will humble themselves and pray, and seek My face and turn from their wicked
ways, then I will hear from heaven, and will forgive their sin
and will heal their land.

—2 Chronicles 7:14

Praying Like Priests

Being effective ambassadors of our mystery nation without interceding for those around us is impossible. That is the essence of our
task. I read a quote before I became a pastor many years ago: "The
man who mobilizes the Christian church to pray will make the
greatest contribution to world evangelization in history."[6] Taking
that to heart, my very first act as a young pastor was to establish a
team of intercessors. We met weekly, laid the map of our city on the
floor, and walked on it as we declared, "Every place on which our foot
shall tread, You have given to us!" We prayed that there would be a
divine boomerang on evil and that everything meant for our harm
would be turned for our good.

One day a woman came to me very upset because an adult book-
store had opened in her neighborhood. We immediately began interceding against the spirit behind pornography and that store. We
didn't know a lot about spiritual warfare back then, but we daily
drove by that establishment and commanded it to go in Jesus's name!
We knew it was important to pluck up satanic seeds before they grew
deep roots that required much more prayer labor. So we prayed for
that business to fail.

Do you know what happened? Within two weeks the porn shop
closed, and the shop was sold to a print company. That printer became
the printer for our church, printing our tracts, bulletins, and news-
letters. The owner ended up joining the mystery nation by receiving
Jesus Christ as his personal Lord and Savior and becoming an active
part of our church. Not only that, as long as I served as pastor in that
community, not one adult business opened in our township. Not one.

We have amazing power as citizens of this mystery nation. Pray
for your city, and prophesy *to* your city. That is your priestly duty

in these end times. Everywhere you walk you carry the power of another world!

Our church grew from one hundred twenty-five members to nearly three thousand within six years. The city knew about us. Police departments began calling us for prayer. Judges involved in tough cases called us to pray for them. We even received calls from people who told us that their doctors referred them to us for prayer.

While other communities in Michigan were losing manufacturing and it looked as though our city would be next, God worked a miracle and brought one of the largest manufacturing plants to our community through a series of people working together who did not even know that a church was praying for them. The whole thing was so miraculous, it was turned into an award-winning documentary film called *Second Shift*.[7]

No matter who you are, if you are a member of the mystery nation, you have more power than you can imagine. The key is to use it.

A Special Mark of Protection for Intercessors

In Ezekiel 9 God instructed an angel to place a mark on those who cry out for their city (Ezek. 9:4–6). Could it be that God has designed a special mark to protect those who are calling out to Him on behalf of others and on behalf of their cities? I believe so.

My successor at Mount Hope Church, Pastor Kevin Berry, began an annual "Breakthrough Lansing" intercessory prayer meeting. In 2015 I counted nearly thirty local pastors participating. Not all of them share the same eschatological outlook, yet we had beautiful harmony in the Holy Spirit as we prayed together for our nation and our city. Lansing's mayor attended the meeting and allowed the intercessors to lay hands on him and pray for him.

As priests we must intercede for our nation: "It is written, 'My house shall be called a house of prayer'" (Matt. 21:13). Threats are all around us. If we don't rise up as priestly intercessors, the threats will furiously escalate. God's protective hedge has kept us from harm more times than we know. But if we continue to offend Him without repentance and fail to intercede, the hedge will weaken, just as Israel's did when the people turned their backs on God. It's time for this mystery nation to arise and intercede because the future depends on it!

As citizens of the mystery nation, our defense forces are supernatural.

> For though we walk in the flesh, we do not war according to the flesh. For the weapons of our warfare are not carnal, but mighty through God to the pulling down of strongholds, casting down imaginations and every high thing that exalts itself against the knowledge of God, bringing every thought into captivity to the obedience of Christ.
>
> —2 Corinthians 10:3–5

We, as citizens of the mystery nation, can expect God to guide us, lead us, propel us, and protect us in the days ahead.

Are you afraid of opposition? Do you doubt you can succeed under difficult circumstances? Don't believe lies. Paul the apostle established churches under the oppressive Roman government. The church grew to a point where, after just thirty years, the entire known world had heard the gospel (Col. 1:5–6). Jesus promised that "not a hair of your head shall perish" (Luke 21:18).

Prayers Will be Answered in the Tribulation

Some wonder if prayer will stop working during the final *shabua*, the Tribulation period. The Book of Revelation shows that intercessory prayers we engage in now will continue to be answered, even during the time of the Tribulation (5:8; 8:3–4). Imagine the prayers you pray now for loved ones and friends being used by God to save them during the Tribulation. What a powerful thing!

Too many of God's people have settled for less than He intended because they don't realize the power available to them. Some stop far short. In my practical pastoral ministries class, I would always ask the ministry students to list fifty things they wanted in their lives, families, and ministries. Over 90 percent could not complete a list of fifty things they hoped for. As members of the mystery nation, agents of the other world, and ambassadors of God's kingdom, we must have greater hope daily so we can constantly offer more hope to people around us.

> Now to Him who is able to do exceedingly abundantly beyond all that we ask or imagine, according to the power that works in us, to Him be the glory in the church and in Christ Jesus throughout all generations, forever and ever. Amen.
>
> —Ephesians 3:20–21

Ambassadors Speak What Their King Speaks

Hope comes when we speak the hope given to us by God. As Solomon wrote, "Death and life are in the power of the tongue, and those who love it will eat its fruit" (Prov. 18:21).

A man in our church owned a great business that started suffering during an economic downturn. The man took an unorthodox approach: he told God he would speak only words of faith and would quit listening to radio and television newscasts. Since that time his business has seen remarkable growth.

As agents of God on earth, we must realize and take seriously that the words we speak will create an environment of some kind—either for increase or for decrease, for victory or for defeat, for health or for sickness, for wealth or for scarcity. Words create or destroy.

In Ezekiel 37 God showed the prophet a pile of dry bones. He didn't say, "Go buy some glue and put these bones back together." No, God said to speak to the bones, prophesy to them. That is when the bones began supernaturally coming back together (Ezek. 37:1–7). If we do the speaking and decreeing on earth for our King, He will work the miracles, whether in marriages, businesses, churches, or nations.

Ambassador, rise up and speak up! As ambassadors of another kingdom, we are allowed to speak with supernatural power, not our opinions, but what our King speaks. We cannot afford to speak our own opinions or parrot the scoffers. When a reporter asks, "How do you feel about the gay marriage decision?" or "What's your opinion of the abortion issue?" I respond, "Since I am an ambassador of another nation, I am only permitted to say the exact same thing as my King says about those matters." Jesus Himself will work with us miraculously if we let Him.

> Then they went forth and preached everywhere, the Lord working with them and confirming the word through the accompanying signs.
>
> —Mark 16:20

The professing church today is heading in two opposite directions. Some are sliding into political correctness, a social agenda, and a false ecumenicalism (calling it unity). The second group is advancing deeper into God's Word, God's plan, and dependence on the Holy Spirit. I choose that direction!

As citizens of a holy nation, we march to the beat of God's drum, not the beat of modern culture. We must once again become the conscience of our culture by teaching the doctrine of Christ as the first-century church did. They obeyed God rather than man and responded to the Holy Spirit rather than what was popular (Acts 5:29).

These early believers, first-century citizens of the mystery nation, filled their cities with biblical teaching, even bringing conviction on powerful leaders who ordered them not to teach in Jesus's name (Acts 5:28; Col. 1:25–27).

Secrets from heaven are now coming to earth. Plans from the heart of God, fresh prophetic light, wisdom, knowledge, dreams, visions, and revelations are being released to those who walk with God intimately—those who know they are citizens of the mystery nation.

An Imam Joins the Mystery Nation

More than twenty years ago, I had the privilege of teaching a practical pastoral ministries class at the Mount Hope training institute. A young African student, Anthony, had recently accepted Christ and been delivered from a satanic cult in Ghana. Anthony graduated from our training school, and some of our daughter churches sent him back to Africa and supported him to plant a church in West Africa.

Things were slow at first, but something happened after six years of ministry. Hundreds then thousands started coming to Christ and attending Anthony's disciple-making ministry. In the next ten years, three hundred more churches were established, including a six-thousand-member, French-speaking congregation made up mostly of former Muslims.

In early 2010 Anthony met a former Islamic imam who shared an amazing story with him. He had been dying with cancer and getting increasingly weaker. He flew to Mecca, where supposedly the best hospital and treatment were available. They couldn't treat him and said he might have just a few days to live.

He was carried aboard a plane to take him home to Africa to die. On the plane he saw a passenger reading a Christian book about Jesus healing. After arriving at the hospital in Africa, the imam was wheeled into a special room to die. He could no longer move in his own power. That night he prayed, "Jesus, I saw the words 'Jesus heals' on a book a man was reading. If You heal me in the next two days, I'll leave Islam and serve You the rest of my days."

That night he experienced what he thought was a dream. When he awoke, he crawled out of bed on his own volition and went to the bathroom. His wife started screaming. He told her of the dream he had that Jesus came into the room and walked up to him and said, "You asked me to heal you, so I have come to do it." Jesus laid His hand on the imam and left. He thought it had been a dream, but it was real.

Now a follower of Jesus Christ, this former imam is a member of the mystery nation, traveling everywhere telling people that Jesus is real and He is Lord. This man usually cannot stay more than thirty minutes in any one place because of the threats on his life.

Reaching One Hundred Thousand

Being a citizen and representative of the mystery nation is no small thing, especially as the days grow darker. You are now in a partnership with God through His Son Jesus Christ. Instead of working *for* His kingdom, you are working *from* His kingdom and bringing hope and a refreshing new life to every desert place you go.

In my early years as a pastor, I prayed that God would help me plant a hundred Mount Hope churches with a combined attendance of at least one hundred thousand. I hoped that with God's help I would see that achieved before my time as pastor was finished. Sometimes I felt like I had failed. But God always knows something we don't. Success often looks like failure at first.

I worked hard to train pastors. The Mount Hope Bible Training Institute and church planter's school trained hundreds of ministerial candidates. But it looked like my prayer wasn't going to be answered and my dream would not be fulfilled, at least not during my time as pastor. I began to wonder if my dream had been too massive. We had managed to plant and launch forty-three daughter and satellite churches. Our church had grown from a handful to three thousand in attendance within six years. Because of this, I was often invited to speak at various leadership and church-growth venues.

One of those venues was in San Diego. Pastors, evangelists, and missionaries attended from around the world. After I had spoken, a man from the Philippines approached me and thanked me for planting a Mount Hope Church in Iloilo, Philippines. This was our first church plant in another country. He then told me about the growth of our church in the Philippines and how it had planted two hundred more churches from the original one. When I heard those words, inside I jumped for joy. I had no idea that much had happened in the fifteen years since we launched that church.

When I returned to Lansing, I contacted our missions director, Bruce Van Hal, and asked him to do some research for me. I wanted to know how many churches we now had in our Mount Hope network, including our daughter and granddaughter churches, as well as our satellite churches. And I wanted to know the combined total Sunday attendance. When he delivered his report to me, I shouted praise to God for His wonderful grace. The report showed that we had not just forty-three churches in Michigan, but more than two hundred in Asia and three hundred in Africa, with a combined Sunday attendance of more than one hundred thousand!

Who could have imagined that what started out as a small church in Lansing would grow to more than one hundred thousand members globally? God is able to do exceedingly abundantly above all that we ask or think, although it may be in different ways than we originally expected.

As members of the mystery nation, we engage in authoritative prayer by speaking what God speaks and making decrees over our families, churches, cities, and nation. I remember meeting with our deacons and elders during an economic downturn and telling them, "We are not going to think survival—we are going to think and speak increase and abundance." From that day forward, we spoke the prophetic revelation of acceleration and advancement of the kingdom of God in our generation. After all, we are agents of a powerful mystery nation.

Ambassadors Called Home

The day will come when all the ambassadors of the mystery nation will suddenly be recalled to their home country. Before any war a nation calls its ambassadors home from the foreign land. Before the final *shabua*, when the wrath of God is poured out, He is going to call us home as followers of Christ. No wonder Paul called the Rapture "the blessed hope" (Titus 2:13).

Chapter 9

THE GREAT SECRET REVEALED

THE MYSTERY OF THE DISAPPEARANCE OF MILLIONS

> Listen, I tell you a mystery: We shall not all sleep, but we
> shall all be changed. In a moment, in the twinkling of an
> eye, at the last trumpet, for the trumpet will sound, the
> dead will be raised incorruptible, and we shall be changed.
> —1 CORINTHIANS 15:51–52

SOMEONE ONCE SAID, "When the end of the world comes, I want to be in Cincinnati because it's always twenty years behind the times."[1] Well, I have news for you. A moment is coming—we don't know the day or the hour—when a trumpet will blast and in a twinkling of an eye the dead in Christ will rise to meet Jesus in the air (1 Thess. 4:16–18). Then the followers of Christ who are alive on the earth will be caught up to meet them and Jesus in the air, and from that moment on, we will be with the Lord forever. This is the mysterious event that signals the end of the church age. It will be the first phase of Christ's coming, and it will take untold millions by surprise.

You see, we are living right now in a parenthetical period called the church age or the age of grace. God has extended His hand of mercy through Jesus Christ to invite everyone who accepts Him to be part of His heavenly family. Some are accepting that invitation, but many are ignoring it. But an end to the age of grace is coming.

The disciples asked Jesus, "What will be the sign of Your coming and of the end of the age?" (Matt. 24:3). Notice they didn't say "the end of the world." The Bible doesn't talk about the end of the world, as pop culture and apocalyptic movies do, but rather about the end of the age. This age will conclude dramatically and globally with the Rapture. Paul described it in 1 Thessalonians: "For the Lord Himself will descend from heaven with a shout, with the voice of the archangel, and with the trumpet call of God. And the dead in Christ will rise first. Then we who are alive and remain shall be *caught up* together with them in the clouds to meet the Lord in the air. And so we shall be forever with the Lord" (4:16–17, emphasis added).

The Greek word for *caught up*, *harpazō*, means "to catch up or snatch away with sudden force." In the Latin Vulgate it is translated as *raptus*, from which we get the word *rapture*. Picture a high-powered electromagnet and a steel ball. When you turn on the electromagnet, the steel ball pops up due to magnetic attraction. That is what the Rapture is going to be like—sudden, instantaneous, irreversible, and powerful. That is why Scripture describes it as being like a thief in the night (1 Thess. 5:2; 2 Pet. 3:10). Jesus is not a thief—He is taking what belongs to Him, His people—but the way a thief snatches things quickly and by surprise is how the Rapture will take place.

I believe it is quite likely our generation will experience the Rapture. Jesus promised us this blessed hope, which He described in John 14, saying, "I will come again and receive you to Myself" (v. 3). The coming of Christ is imminent. He could come for His church at any moment.

Jesus said, "As were the days of Noah, so will be the coming of the Son of Man" (Matt. 24:37). Noah told his unrighteous neighbors for 120 years what was coming, and still they went about their everyday business thinking only of themselves. Selfishness, sin, evil imaginations, and violence characterized Noah's day. So we know those signs will also lead up to the end of the age. Jesus said, "Now learn this lesson from the fig tree: When its branch becomes tender and grows leaves, you know that summer is near. So also, when you shall see all these things, you know that it is near, even at the doors" (Matt. 24:32–33).

The signs we see taking place—earthquakes, famine, and pestilence in various parts of the world—are coming together in a concentrated, intensified way. Jesus said, "Truly I say to you, this generation will not pass away until all these things take place" (Matt. 24:34). The final generation will see the convergence of all the end-time signs.

We may now be living in the generation when Christians will be changed in the twinkling of an eye. We will be a part of the first resurrection. When the trumpet sounds and the dead in Christ rise, we will rise up to meet them in the air and forever be with the Lord.

The Rapture will catch a great many people up—and catch a great many people by surprise. Those of us living in Christ have nothing to fear. Jesus said a beautiful thing in Luke 21:28: "When these things begin to happen, look up and lift up your heads, for your redemption is drawing near." We should not be bowed down with anxiety as we anticipate this wonderful event. Rather, we should lift our heads high with hope!

Two Trumpets

Some people confuse the Rapture with Jesus's second coming. Let me be clear: they are two separate events that take place at least seven years apart. The Rapture is *not* the Second Coming but the initial phase of the Second Coming. The Rapture and Christ's return do not happen simultaneously. Notice that the Bible says that for the Rapture, Jesus is coming in the air, not to the earth (1 Thess. 4:17). Believers will join Him in the air. At least seven years later, at Armageddon, He'll return to the earth in His second coming.

Why does the catching away of the church happen first? Because, as Paul wrote, believers are not appointed to experience God's wrath (1 Thess. 5:9). Before dealing with a wicked world, God will remove the Christians. We see this pictured in the Old Testament when Lot and his family were removed before judgment fell on Sodom. Enoch was raptured before the Flood. Noah and his family were safely secured in the ark before the Flood came. Likewise, you and I, as believers, will be in heaven before those final, terrible seven years of agony on earth begin.

Keep in mind that not all church members and professing believers will be raptured. The Rapture is reserved for those who have truly been born again, have been walking with God, and are presently doing the will of God. Jesus put it this way: "Not everyone who says to Me, 'Lord, Lord,' shall enter the kingdom of heaven, but he who does the will of My Father who is in heaven" (Matt. 7:21). We can't just casually say the name of Jesus and get a free entry pass. We must be doing the will of our heavenly Father too—orthodoxy plus orthopraxy.

The Rapture will end the parenthetical church age. Most people are surprised to learn that this is not the first time people have been caught up to heaven, and it won't be the last. There are several raptures in the Bible. For example, in Genesis 5:24 Enoch was caught up to heaven and was never seen on earth again. In 2 Kings 2:11 Elijah went to be with God without dying. Jesus Himself ascended into heaven in Acts 1:9–11. In the future, during the final *shabua*, the two witnesses will be caught up to heaven after they are killed and then raised from the dead after their bodies have lain in the streets of Jerusalem for three and a half days (Rev. 11:11–12). Then, at the end of the final *shabua*, Jesus will send His angels to gather the elect—those who refused the mark of the beast and accepted Christ during the Tribulation (Matt. 24:31).

The Rapture of the church closes the church age. Then, after some initial chaos, confusion, and a transition period, the world will enter the dreaded Tribulation, an hour of supreme agony for those who miss the Rapture.

Two trumpets are spoken of in Scripture. Some people think that the trumpet Paul wrote about in 1 Corinthians 15 is the same as the last trumpet of Revelation. It's not. They are two different trumpets. The first trumpet is a "ready, set" trumpet, and the second trumpet means, "Go!" Numbers 10 shows us:

> And the Lord spoke to Moses, saying: Make for yourself two silver trumpets. Of a hammered work you will make them, and you will use them for summoning of the assembly and directing the breaking up of the camps. When they blow

both of them, all the assembly will assemble themselves to
you at the door of the tent of meeting.

—Numbers 10:1–3

The first trumpet and the last trumpet were both assembly trumpets, but they meant different things. The first trumpet meant, "Get
ready to move out of camp!" The second trumpet meant, "We're
leaving immediately!" Ready, set, go!

I believe we have already heard the first trumpet, which is a spiritual awakening. In the last thirty years, we have been experiencing
the greatest spiritual awakening in all of human history. Many millions of people are being swept into the kingdom in places like China,
Russia, Latin America, and Africa. It's happening all over the world.
In my view we are living in the time between the trumpets, so to
speak. The next trumpet that blows will be what Paul called the last
trumpet, and in the twinkling of an eye, all believers will be changed
and will vanish from the earth.

> We shall not all sleep, but we shall all be changed. In a
> moment, in the twinkling of an eye, at the last trumpet, for
> the trumpet will sound, the dead will be raised incorrupt-
> ible, and we shall be changed. For this corruptible will put
> on incorruption, and this mortal will put on immortality.
> When this corruptible will have put on incorruption, and
> this mortal will have put on immortality, then the saying
> that is written shall come to pass: "Death is swallowed up
> in victory."

—1 Corinthians 15:51–54

What happens then? For those of us caught up in the air and those
who remain on earth, it will be two very different stories.

Marriage Supper

When believers die, their spirits go immediately into the presence
of the Lord. When the final trumpet sounds, those who have died,

whose bodies are in the ground and whose spirits are in heaven, will be reunited with their bodies. God knows where every piece of DNA is, and He will recreate each person. Better than that, He will give us incorruptible bodies in place of corruptible ones (1 Cor. 15:53). We will become like Jesus (Phil. 3:21)!

When Jesus rose from the dead, He had a resurrected body. So will we. Mortality will put on immortality. The dead in Christ will no longer be spirits in heaven but have glorified bodies too wonderful to presently imagine. Then the rest of the believers who are still alive on earth will be changed. We will meet the others in the air and our bodies will be transformed and glorified as theirs are. What a day!

As the world below enters its final *shabua*, believers in heaven will be experiencing two events foretold in Scripture. First we will go to the judgment seat of Christ to receive our millennial assignments and our rewards (2 Cor. 5:10). Jesus will tenderly say things such as, "I want to thank you for receiving Me as Savior," "I want to thank you for being a light to that person in your workplace," "Thanks for ministering to those in prison and on your street," and "Thanks for even the smallest kindness you did in My name." He will give each one of us what we are due.

At this judgment there will be no condemnation because there is no condemnation to those who are in Christ (Rom. 8:1). Rather, we will receive rewards and crowns of righteousness. Paul promised that there is a crown of righteousness laid up for all who look for His appearing (2 Tim. 4:8). What do people with crowns do? They rule! We will then get our millennial positions in preparation for serving on earth with Jesus for a thousand years (Rev. 20:4).

But first there's a celebratory feast! The Bible tells us we will attend the marriage supper of the Lamb, where we become the bride of Christ, what He always intended us to be. We will be eating and delighting and dancing on the sea of glass. You may have attended some extravagant weddings in your life, but this will be an event for the ages. You don't want to miss it.

Is it any wonder that Jesus said, "Let not your heart be troubled" and "Lift up your heads, for your redemption is drawing near" (John 14:1; Luke 21:28)? We don't have to fear! Those who are walking with Jesus have it made. We don't have a single thing to worry about. When we look around at the perplexing problems in this world, we are tempted to be distraught and troubled. But when we look up, hope and excitement floods our souls.

Aftermath on Earth

The scene on earth will be very different. Everyone who refused to confess Jesus Christ as Lord and Savior and did not do the will of God will be stuck in a nightmare scenario. Think about the mother who had no time for God personally, but took her children to church faithfully—one day her children won't be coming home. Think about the father who dismissed God and didn't want to become a "Jesus freak." One day he will come home and his wife will be gone.

Confusion will be rampant. Sudden chaos will grip the whole world as a result of the great catching away, the Rapture. The only thing keeping full-fledged evil from overwhelming the earth right now, we're told in 2 Thessalonians 2:6–7, is the presence of the Holy Spirit in God's people. Suddenly, in a moment, that restraining influence will be gone.

Some teach that all babies and children will be taken to heaven in the Rapture. However, if you study the history of the judgments of God from Genesis all the way through Revelation, it's plain: children of unbelievers always suffered with their parents. This is not to say they wouldn't go to heaven upon death, just that the Rapture is reserved for godly believers and their children. God didn't take the babies out of Sodom and Gomorrah before fire rained down (Gen. 19). When Achan was judged for stealing treasure for himself, Achan's children were destroyed along with Achan and his wife (Josh. 7).

The good news is that if a child has a believing mother or father, the child will be caught up in the Rapture (1 Cor. 7:14). If not, the child will likely stay on earth. It's that simple. It's the way everything has worked in the past. To see how God will do something in the future, look to how He did it in the past. Children, of course, still go to heaven if they die as children—God is merciful. But to think that all the nurseries and maternity wards are going to be emptied by the Rapture and all pregnant women will suddenly become unpregnant, as some teach, is inconsistent with the rule: how God fulfilled prophecy in the past is how He will fulfill prophecy in the future.

How will people on earth respond? Some undoubtedly will say, "I'm glad all those religious nuts are gone." Some may suggest that those who vanished were not of earth's harmony and had to be removed in order for the planet to enter the utopian new world order. Meanwhile, the Antichrist will rise quickly and offer plausible explanations of where all the people went. And suddenly twenty-one rapid-fire judgments will begin to pour out on the earth (Rev. 6–19).

Dealing With Israel

For Israel the end of the church age is highly significant. God is reengaging Israel as a nation for the first time since Jesus rode into Jerusalem on a donkey. The Bible makes it clear that God is not finished with Israel as a nation.

The Jewish religious leaders in Jesus's day did not understand that His coming would be in two parts, a first coming and a second coming. At the first coming, the Messiah was born in a manger in Bethlehem, lived a sinless life, was executed, rose from the dead, ascended to heaven, and said, "I'll come back again." But they didn't understand who He was. They paid attention only to the scriptures about the conquering Messiah and filtered out the scriptures about the humble Messiah. They wanted their King to ride on a horse, brandishing a sword and leading an army. Jesus will do that the second time He comes, but for the first coming, Jesus said, "You did not know the time of your visitation" (Luke 19:44).

I was raised in a church where the pastor taught us that God hates Jews and is forever done with the Jewish people because they rejected Jesus. This pastor said they were cursed forever and there was no hope for Israel. That is so contrary to the clear teaching of Scripture.

Romans 11 tells us plainly that God is not done with the Jewish nation. He loves Israel like He loves you and me, but His direct dealings with them stopped during the church age. During that parenthetical period He raised up another nation—the mystery nation, the church—and is using them to provoke the Jews to jealousy. This will happen in growing measure in the days ahead both before and after the Rapture. When all believers are caught away, God will once again turn to Israel as His nation.

Different Views of When

There are four basic viewpoints on when the Rapture will occur. All viewpoints affirm that Jesus is coming for His church, but they differ on when.

Pretribulation Rapture

The church will be taken off the earth prior to the seven-year *shabua* spoken of by Jeremiah, Daniel, Jesus, and John. This is my view. It is the only position in complete harmony with the doctrine of imminence—that Jesus will come suddenly, at an unspecified time, to gather His people. (See Matthew 24:36, 42–44; Mark 13:32–37; Luke 17:26–30, 34–36.)

Pretribulation Rapture View

Second Coming of
Jesus Christ

Abomination of
Desolation

PRETRIBULATION
Rapture

Seven-Year Tribulation
Final *Shabua*

Midtribulation Rapture

The midtribulation Rapture view teaches that the church will be taken off the earth when the Antichrist, the magnetic world leader, moves his image into the temple. To hold the midtribulation Rapture view, you must also ignore the clear biblical teachings that Jesus could come at any moment. We know the precise midpoint of the Tribulation period will be when the Antichrist moves his own image into the rebuilt temple in Jerusalem and begins his rampage against the Jewish people and those who worship Jesus (Dan. 9:27; 2 Thess. 2:4; Rev. 12:6).

Midtribulation Rapture View

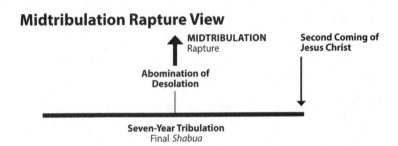

Posttribulation Rapture

The posttribulation view claims that all Christians will go through the time of God's wrath on the earth and then be raptured as Jesus returns to earth in His second coming. To accept the posttribulation Rapture position, you must totally reject the doctrine of imminence, since we would know when Christ's return will occur at Armageddon and could easily calculate the number of days from the time the Antichrist claims himself to be God and moves his image into the rebuilt temple (Dan. 12:11).

Posttribulation Rapture View

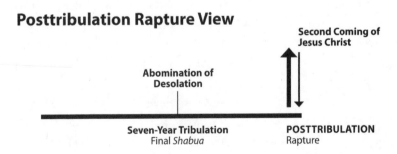

Pre-wrath Rapture

The pre-wrath Rapture view suggests that Jesus will leave His church on the earth until God's wrath begins, but we don't know precisely when the actual wrath begins during the final *shabua*. The pre-wrath Rapture position does project a certain element of imminence; however, that element only goes into effect after the Tribulation begins and the Antichrist has already been revealed. In effect, this position limits the "at any moment" teaching of Jesus, Paul, and Peter (Matt. 24:36, 42–44; Mark 13:32–37; Luke 17:26–36; 1 Thess. 5:2; 2 Pet. 3:10).

Pre-Wrath Rapture View

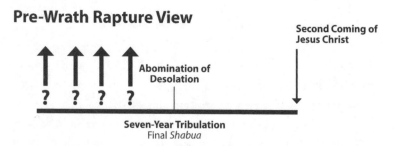

Encroachment on the Doctrine of Imminence

We must, however, never let differing viewpoints become places of division; instead, they should be opportunities for sincere discussion. Our fellowship should never rest on when we believe the Rapture will take place. All four of these positions are held by true believers. We are known by our love one for another, not by our beliefs concerning when the Rapture will occur. As Jesus said, "By this all men will know that you are My disciples, if you have love for one another" (John 13:35).

We must remember that authentic believers may hold differing views on matters of eschatology. We must never attack the sincerity of fellow believers because they take a different position on eschatology. I have friends who are posttributionists and even some who are amillenialists, yet they love Jesus. The problem is that some eschatological viewpoints sometimes lead to bad decisions, such as accepting the deception that the church has taken the place of Israel (replacement theology). Some who adhere to aberrant eschatology have become anti-Israel. And without a pretribulation Rapture, you have no "Christ could come at any moment" doctrine.

With that clearly said, I do believe there is a deceptive attack on the imminence of the Rapture—that is, that Jesus will catch us away at any time. A great myth has been loosed on the church that says a man named John Darby invented the doctrine of the Rapture back in the 1800s.[2] That is simply not true. During the first four hundred years of church history, the church fathers, including Barnabas, Tertullian, and Irenaeus, taught that Jesus would come for His people before the Antichrist would be revealed on the earth.[3] For example, Ephraem, a Syrian church father, wrote around AD 370, "For all the saints and Elect of God are gathered, prior to the Tribulation that is to come, and are taken to the Lord lest they see the confusion that is to overwhelm the world because of our sins."[4]

Some critics of belief in the pretribulation Rapture of the church say it is escapist theology for people with no interest in confronting the world's challenges. I will point out that it was Jesus who promised an escape: "Therefore watch always and pray that you may be counted worthy to escape all these things that will happen and to stand before the Son of Man" (Luke 21:36).

And the apostle Paul told us some would *not* escape: "When they say, 'Peace and safety!' then sudden destruction will come upon them as labor upon a woman with child, and they shall not escape" (1 Thess. 5:3). Believing in a pretribulation Rapture is not for people wanting to escape trouble. It is for people who take Scripture at face value. Here are several reasons I believe the Rapture will take place before the Tribulation.

It's in the Greek text.

Revelation 3:10 reads, "I also will keep you from the hour of temptation which shall come upon the entire world, to test those who dwell on the earth." The word *from* in the Greek is *ek*, which means "out of,"[5] not "safe through." So Jesus is saying, "I will keep you out of the hour of temptation," a reference to the coming Tribulation.

We won't be punished with the world system.

The judgments of the tribulation are called the "wrath of the Lamb" (Rev. 6:16). The church is not the object of Christ's wrath. In fact, Paul stated strongly that there is no condemnation for those who are in Christ Jesus (Rom. 8:1). Jesus is not going to beat up His bride in the "wrath of the Lamb" judgments. We are to be a glorious church without spot or wrinkle, a beautiful bride for Christ.

Jesus spoke of escape.

As we already noted, Jesus told His followers to watch and pray that they would escape the things that are coming on the earth (Luke 21:36). Paul warned that most will not escape (1 Thess. 5:3).

Something must unleash the restrained lawlessness referenced in 2 Thessalonians 2:1–11.

That which is currently restraining the lawless one can only be the influence of the Holy Spirit through the church that is both salt and light in this world (Matt. 5:13–14).

The church disappears for most of Revelation.

Revelation 2–3 tell us about the church age. In Revelation 3 Jesus said, "I have set before you an open door, and no one can shut it....Because you have kept My word of patience, I also will keep you from the hour of temptation which shall come upon the entire world, to test those who dwell on the earth" (Rev. 3:8, 10).

Right after that, in Revelation 4, we read: "After this I looked. And there was an open door in heaven. The first voice I heard was like a trumpet speaking with me, saying, 'Come up here, and I will show you things which must take place after this'" (v. 1). Immediately you find the church in heaven. There is no mention of the church in Revelation 6–19. The only "church" on earth is the harlot church, the church of apostasy, the church that has morally and doctrinally left the faith.

The Greek phrase at the beginning of Revelation 4:1 is *meta tauta*, meaning "after this." Now we ask, after what? The answer is after the things of the church age in chapters 2–3. That is why the church is never pictured as being on the earth until after the Second Coming near the end of Revelation.

After the church leaves the earth, God begins His direct dealings with Israel again. One hundred forty-four thousand Jewish Christians are sealed to take the gospel to the whole world. Nowhere in Revelation does it say that all Christians or the church will be sealed or preserved on earth during the Tribulation.

Terminology changes to Hebrew.

Revelation 1–5 is written in Gentile or church terminology for believers of every nation, every tongue, and every tribe. But when we get to chapter 6, when the Tribulation begins, the writing once again begins using Hebrew terminology and figures. This is because in Revelation 6 we see the start of the Tribulation, the time of God's direct and decisive dealing with the nation of Israel once again. It's the final *shabua*, Daniel's seventieth week.

Jesus is preparing a place for us.

Jesus said, "If I go and prepare a place for you, I will come again and receive you to Myself" (John 14:3). If we are going to be raptured at the end of the Tribulation, why is Jesus bothering to prepare a place for us? If He is coming back to earth to rule with us for one thousand years, why is He bothering to prepare us a place right now? It's because during the Tribulation, Christians will be in heaven.

We don't know the day or hour.

Jesus said, "Concerning that day and hour no one knows" (Matt. 24:36). How can that be if the angel told Daniel from the time the Antichrist moves his image into the temple there will be 1,290 days (1,260 days until Jesus comes and 30 days of earth cleanup)? Because when Jesus said we don't know the day or the hour, He wasn't talking about His second coming. He was talking about the Rapture of believers. (See Matthew 24:36, 50; 25:13.)

Jesus gave comfort.

Why did Jesus say, "Let not your heart be troubled" (John 14:1, 27)? How could Paul say to "comfort one another with these words" about the end times (1 Thess. 4:18)? How can we look at what's coming in the Tribulation and comfort one another with those words? What kind of comfort is it to know that there will be a financial crash, a man arising who makes Hitler look like a Sunday school teacher, and another holocaust?

Think of it this way too: Did God love Noah more than He loves you? God sealed Noah up in an ark before the judgment. Did God love Lot more than He loves you? Lot was not even a very good witness. An angel had to grab him by the arm and take him out before the judgment came. But God made sure His people got out first. That is an example of the kind of comfort we can have when knowing such difficult times are coming upon the earth.

No instructions were left.

Why didn't Jesus or Paul or Peter or John give the church instructions on what to do during the Tribulation? Jesus never told us to look for the Antichrist or watch out for Armageddon. He told believers to look for His coming and be ready at any moment (Matt. 24:44; 2 Tim. 4:8).

God is not a God of delay.

Notice what Jesus said about the servant who says the Lord is going to delay His coming.

> But if that servant says in his heart, "My master delays his coming,"…the master of that servant will come on a day when he does not look for him, and at an hour when he is not aware, and will cut him to pieces and will appoint him his portion with the unbelievers.
>
> —Luke 12:45–46

The Lord called that servant evil who says Jesus will delay His coming. But He said the one watching for His coming at any moment will be blessed (Luke 12:43–44).

It leads to good fruit.

The greatest soul winners I know teach that the Rapture is imminent, and some of the best Christian organizations believe the same thing. Having a right view of the future of the earth and of the church seems to go a long way to energizing our work now.

Third Day Theory

Let's talk about one more Rapture-specific idea that has to do with the "third day" spoken of in Scripture. Hosea 6:2 tells us, "After two days He will revive us. On the third day He will raise us up, that we may live before Him."

We find a mention of the third day in Exodus as well:

> The LORD said to Moses, "Go to the people and sanctify them today and tomorrow, and have them wash their clothes, and be ready for the third day, for on the third day the LORD will come down in the sight of all the people on Mount Sinai."…So on the third day, in the morning, there was thunder and lightning, and a thick cloud on the mountain, and the sound of an exceedingly loud trumpet.… Then Moses brought the people out of the camp to meet with God, and they stood at the foot of the mountain. Now Mount Sinai was completely covered in smoke because the LORD had descended upon it in fire.… When the sound of the trumpet grew louder and louder, Moses spoke, and God answered him with a voice. The LORD came down on Mount Sinai, on the top of the mountain.
>
> —EXODUS 19:10–11, 16–20

In John 2:1–2 we learn that "on the third day there was a wedding in Cana of Galilee. The mother of Jesus was there. Both Jesus and

His disciples were invited to the wedding." Psalm 90:4 tells us, "For a thousand years in Your sight are but as yesterday when it is past, or as a night watch in the night time." Second Peter 3:8 affirms, "But, beloved, do not be ignorant of this one thing, that with the Lord one day is as a thousand years, and a thousand years as one day."

What this all *may* point to is this: a third day resurrection for the church! Jesus was raised from the dead early on the third day, and so the spiritual body of Christ, that mystery nation, the church, may be raised up early on her third day. If a day is as a thousand years, we could already be early in the third day. We don't know, but it fits the present world scenario and may be another sign for us to pay attention to. You may miss a plane, train, or bus, but don't miss the Rapture.

Chapter 10

THE FINAL *SHABUA*

EARTH'S INESCAPABLE HOUR OF AGONY AND DISTRESS

For then will be great tribulation, such as has not happened
since the beginning of the world until now, no, nor ever shall be.
—JESUS, MATTHEW 24:21

AFTER THE RAPTURE millions upon millions of people will be left
on earth, but one man will be far more important than them all.
He is the man of lawlessness spoken of in the Bible, and I believe he
is alive on earth today, waiting in the wings. He is a man with a plan.

This man is the Antichrist—magnetic, charismatic, warm, and
charming. In the Bible he is called the little horn, the lawless one, the
son of perdition, and the beast. Jesus prophesied about him when He
said, "I have come in My Father's name, but you do not receive Me.
If another comes in his own name, you will receive him" (John 5:43).

This man will define the last seven years of human government.
He will personify evil, and the earth will suffer a supreme bloodbath
at his hands. Let's take a closer look at who this man is and what he
will do.

A New Global Leader Arises

Daniel 9:26 refers to the Antichrist as the prince, which is a clear
attempt by the Antichrist to set himself up as the alternative to the
Prince of Peace. The angel told Daniel:

> Then after the sixty-two weeks [of years] the Anointed One
> will be cut off [and denied His Messianic kingdom] and have

nothing [and no one to defend Him], and the people of the
[other] prince who is to come will destroy the city and the
sanctuary. Its end will come with a flood; even to the end
there will be war; desolations are determined.

—Daniel 9:26, AMP

In this verse we are clearly told where the coming world leader
will come from. Notice that he comes from the people who destroy
Jerusalem and the temple. Which people destroyed Jerusalem in
AD 70? It was the Romans. This tells us this man will come from
Europe, most likely from Italy, or at least that's where his operations
will begin. He and his empire are described as a "beast rising out of
the sea" in Revelation 13:1. Consistently throughout prophecy the sea
is used as a symbol of Gentile nations, telling us that this coming
world dictator will emerge from a Gentile nation. (See Daniel 7:3;
Luke 21:25; Revelation 17:1.)

Daniel continues, "And he shall enter into a strong and firm covenant with the many for one week [seven years]" (Dan. 9:27, AMPC).
After the Rapture, which sends the nations into confusion, this world
leader will make a meteoric rise and prove to be a political and military genius. He will swiftly take charge of the New Europe. Jesus
said the people He was speaking to, the Jews, "will receive him," so
we know that most Jews will believe this world leader is their Messiah
or at least Messiah's forerunner. He will lead the people of the whole
world with a political platform of "peace and safety" for a short season
(1 Thess. 5:3). But underlying his rule will be the greatest deception
ever perpetrated on humanity.

What will the Antichrist do? What will happen during his brief
and terrible reign?

He will make peace so the Jewish temple can be restored.

The world will marvel as this man brokers a peace treaty between
Israel and Muslim nations. Nobody has been able to do that since
Israel became a nation again in 1948. This treaty will lead to the
rebuilding of the Jewish temple on its former site. That sounds

impossible because the Dome of the Rock, a Muslim temple, sits there now. But the treaty will allow for the Dome of the Rock and the Jewish temple to share the same Temple Mount. There is plenty of room to rebuild the temple just north of where the Dome of the Rock sits. Believe it or not, the temple will likely go up modularly, so it will be erected in as little as two weeks.

The world will wonder, "How was this man able to stop the violence and bring peace between the Jew and the Muslim?" Everything he does will seem to be the right thing. In their confusion the people of the world will say, "This man can solve all our problems!" (Rev. 13:3–4). Well, yes, he can, but only for a very short season. Then all hell will break loose.

He may have Jewish roots or some apostate Christian background.

The Antichrist may have Jewish roots or be an apostate Christian. How do we know this? Because it says he does not worship the God of his fathers. I believe he may have Jewish roots, because this will make it easier for the Jews to receive him as their Messiah or at least as a forerunner of their Messiah. He may have some connection with apostate Christianity. There is no possibility that the Antichrist will be Muslim as some are suggesting today. No Muslim would dare to claim to be a human deity as the Antichrist eventually will.

He will flatter the world and gain control.

We are told that the Antichrist will be a master of intrigue, using flattery to gain control (Dan. 11:21). He will be a master of deception empowered by the father of lies, Satan. In Daniel 8:24–25 we see that he is a great business genius as well as a political genius. He will become very strong but not by his own power.

> His power shall be mighty, but not by his own power. And he shall destroy wonderfully and shall prosper and practice his will and shall destroy the mighty men and the holy people. By his cunning, he shall cause deceit to succeed under his hand, and he shall magnify himself in his heart.

He shall destroy many in a time of peace. He shall also rise
up against the Prince of princes; but he shall be broken, not
by human hands.

—Daniel 8:24–25

He will bring pseudo economic success.

After the Antichrist makes the peace treaty, bringing a false calm
to the Middle East, the world will enter a brief time of peace and
prosperity. Everybody will seem to be happy. The major confusion
will seem to be over. A false economic prosperity may follow. Then,
near the midpoint of the seven years, this man will implement a cashless society where everybody, according to Revelation 13, must take a
mark on their forehead or their right hand in order to buy or sell. The
nations will give up their autonomy and sovereignty to let this man
rule because he seems to have the magic touch.

I read recently that Sweden is close to being a cashless society. The
article noted that "four out of five purchases in Sweden are made elec-
tronically or by debit card."[1] Other countries are close to becoming
cashless as well.[2] Israel is also studying how to eliminate cash from
its economy.[3] In a cashless society, you no longer need paper money
or credit cards. All you need is something that identifies who you are.

He causes all, both small and great, both rich and poor, both
free and slave, to receive a mark on their right hand or on
their forehead, so that no one may buy or sell, except he
who has the mark or the name of the beast or the number
of his name.

—Revelation 13:16–17

How will this new economy come into place? Possibly as a result
of the crash of the old economy. Something dramatic will have to
happen that causes a currency reset or the widespread acceptance of a
new monetary system that does not use actual money but rather electronic credits. We have already seen a preview sign of this with the
emergence of bitcoins and cybercash.

The Bible further says that the Antichrist will cause "deceit to succeed" (Dan. 8:25). He will also help the working class. Daniel 11:24 says the Antichrist will redistribute wealth, taking from the wealthy and giving to the poor.[4] That is why common people will love him.

> Without warning he will enter the richest areas of the land. Then he will distribute among his followers the plunder and wealth of the rich—something his predecessors had never done. He will plot the overthrow of strongholds, but this will last for only a short while.
>
> —Daniel 11:24, nlt

He will use a religious PR man.

This apparently adorable leader will have a promoter, a PR man the Bible calls the False Prophet. Remember, Satan tries to mimic everything God does, so he will set up an unholy trinity. Satan, the dragon, is the head. The Antichrist is the son, and the False Prophet does the spiritual things (Rev. 13:11–16). This False Prophet will appear to do miracles that promote the world political leader.

He will survive an assassination attempt.

An assassination attempt will be made on the Antichrist, according to Revelation 13:3 and Zechariah 11:17. It will possibly cost him the use of one of his eyes. He will seem to die, and the world will be grieving over him when all of a sudden he will rise up from the dead—an apparent resurrection.

At that point the whole world will worship and adore him, and in so doing, they will actually be worshipping Satan, who is the power behind the man (Rev. 13:4). Why are they able to be deceived? Because they will not love the truth but rather love wickedness. Paul gives this simple explanation:

> Then the lawless one will be revealed…even him, whose coming is in accordance with the working of Satan with all power and signs and false wonders, and with all deception of unrighteousness among those who perish, because they did not receive the love for the truth that they might be saved.

Therefore God will send them a strong delusion, that they
should believe the lie: that they all might be condemned who
did not believe the truth but had pleasure in unrighteousness.

—2 THESSALONIANS 2:8–12

He will emerge in an era known as "the information age."

When will this man arise? How do we know this will happen
soon? Because the angel described what the earth would be like when
the prophecies given to Daniel are unsealed. The angel gave two
very interesting signs. First, "Many shall run to and fro." Literally
this means, "Travel shall be increased." And second, "knowledge
shall increase" (Dan. 12:4). During this era many will also study the
ancient biblical prophecies and draw astounding revelation from the
Holy Spirit.

Let me ask you—is there any better description of the time in
which we live? In all of history there has never been anything like what
we experience now. Transportation has exploded such that people
can go anywhere on the globe within a matter of hours. Never has
there been more knowledge and information understood and applied
by humanity and available to everyone at the touch of a button. None
of this made sense to Daniel at the time. In fact, Daniel admitted this.
The angel told him, "But you, Daniel, shut up the words, and seal the
book" (Dan. 12:4; see also v. 9). How long would it be sealed? "Until
the time of the end" (vv. 4, 9).

The angel was essentially saying, "Daniel, I am giving you these
cryptic messages, and you're not going to understand them, so seal
them up. At a future time they will understand."

The idea of *sealing* is similar to when you seal something in a
Mason jar to preserve its contents. Later you unscrew the lid and pop
the jar open to use its contents. The events described by the angel
were sealed up and not understood until such a time as God unsealed
them—at the time of the end when transportation and knowledge
would dramatically increase. Obviously I believe those times are now.
The angel went on to promise that "the wicked shall do wickedly, and

none of the wicked shall understand, but the wise shall understand"
(Dan. 12:10).

In these times, and especially during the final *shabua*, evil people
will be saying, "I don't understand that Bible stuff. It doesn't make any
sense to me. Throw it away." But wise people—by definition those who
accept the lordship of God through Christ—will have these prophecies unsealed so they understand them. It's a wonderful promise.

Days of Noah

As the Antichrist rules, what kind of atmosphere will prevail on the
earth? Jesus described the characteristics leading to the final *shabua*
as being like the days of Noah:

> Concerning that day and hour no one knows, not even the
> angels of heaven, but My Father only. As were the days of
> Noah, so will be the coming of the Son of Man. For as in the
> days before the flood, they were eating and drinking, mar-
> rying and giving in marriage, until the day Noah entered the
> ark, and did not know until the flood came and took them
> all away, so will be the coming of the Son of Man. Two will
> be in the field; one will be taken, and the other left.
>
> —MATTHEW 24:36–40

In Noah's day people were constantly thinking evil thoughts, and
sin and violence were rampant. We are told in Revelation 9:21 that
this is exactly what the final *shabua* will be like: people won't repent
of their murders, sexual immorality, and magical arts.

Murder includes abortion, sexual immorality includes all kinds of
sexual sin, and magical arts is the word *pharmakeia*, which includes
the use of enchanting drugs. This prophecy could not more accurately
describe our time. Nearly sixty million babies have been aborted
in America since 1973.[5] I never thought I would see a day when
enchanting drugs would be legalized in some states. I never thought I
would see a day when perverted ideas of marriage would be the law of
the land. Yet these things are accepted in society now. The Bible calls

it strong delusion: "Therefore God will send them a strong delusion, that they should believe the lie: that they all might be condemned who did not believe the truth but had pleasure in unrighteousness" (2 Thess. 2:11–12).

Those who consistently reject the truth will fall victim to strong delusion that ultimately leads to the place of the damned. This was the case with the religious leaders in ancient Jerusalem who repeatedly rejected Jesus and finally came to a point where they could not believe (John 12:39). They went beyond the point of no return.

You might ask, is it possible for a God of mercy to give up on people? Paul supplied the answer:

> And since they did not see fit to acknowledge God, God gave them over to a debased mind, to do those things which are not proper. They were filled with all unrighteousness, sexual immorality, wickedness, covetousness, maliciousness; full of envy, murder, strife, deceit. They are gossips, slanderers, God-haters, insolent, proud, boastful, inventors of evil things, and disobedient toward parents, without understanding, covenant breakers, without natural affection, calloused, and unmerciful, who know the righteous requirement of God, that those who commit such things are worthy of death. They not only do them, but also give hearty approval to those who practice them.
>
> —Romans 1:28–32

People have free will and can use it even to commit themselves to death. This passage reads almost like a roll call of the damned. God reached out to these people, but they repeatedly rejected His offer. Drawing from this passage, we see the kind of behavior that will prevail on earth for those seven years. In neighborhoods, at the shopping mall, on television, in schools, and even in the "churches" that remain, the culture will be saturated by this kind of darkness and open wickedness. This is the fruit produced by people who reject God's kingdom rule.

Do you not know that the unrighteous will not inherit the kingdom of God? Do not be deceived. Neither the sexually immoral, nor idolaters, nor adulterers, nor male prostitutes, nor homosexuals, nor thieves, nor covetous, nor drunkards, nor revilers, nor extortioners will inherit the kingdom of God. Such were some of you. But you were washed, you were sanctified, and you were justified in the name of the Lord Jesus by the Spirit of our God.

—1 Corinthians 6:9–11

The Mask Comes Off

During the final *shabua*, when world citizens trust him implicitly, the Antichrist will tear off his mask and reveal his true motive: he wants to be worshipped. Totally possessed by Satan, he becomes the most arrogant, blasphemous person ever to live, and wanting to be God, he moves his image into the newly rebuilt Jewish temple in Jerusalem. Whether this image is a hologram or a statue or something else, he will demand it be worshipped by all. Paul wrote to the Thessalonians:

He will exalt himself and defy everything that people call god and every object of worship. He will even sit in the temple of God, claiming that he himself is God. Don't you remember that I told you about all this when I was with you? And you know what is holding him back, for he can be revealed only when his time comes.

—2 Thessalonians 2:3–6, nlt

This satanically possessed man is a blasphemer of the first order. Daniel talked about his unparalleled arrogance, self-will, blasphemy, and worship of "the god of forces," which I take to mean the occult or possibly military powers (Dan. 7:8; 11:36–38).

When the Antichrist's image is set up in the temple, the Jewish people will realize they have been double-crossed, and that is when many start fleeing Jerusalem as Jesus foretold. Interestingly the Bible assures us that the Jews will eventually come to Jesus Christ (Rom.

11:26). They will discover that Jesus really is their Messiah, and they will make our present-day soul-winning efforts look like a drop in a bucket—such will be their commitment and power. The people of Israel will finally become the light to the world that God always intended them to be.

Trapped on Earth

The last three and a half years of the final *shabua* will feel like hell on earth. It will be like the days of Noah, which seemed like fun—until the rain came. Then God sealed the ark and the floods came up. Not one person survived except Noah and his family, who were in the ark. I imagine people were beating on the door and yelling, "Noah, let us in! Noah, let us in!" Noah could not possibly open the door because Noah never closed the door. God Himself closed and sealed the door of the ark.

So it will be for those trapped on earth: "For then will be great tribulation, such as has not happened since the beginning of the world until now, no, nor ever shall be. Unless those days were shortened, no one would be saved. But for the sake of the elect those days will be shortened" (Matt. 24:21–22). You think times are tough now. At that time one relentless judgment after another will hit the planet—twenty-one in all. Fires will destroy massive regions and forests. A third of the freshwater supply will become toxic, poisoned. Many people will suffer strange boils on their skin. Meteors will pass close to the earth, causing debris to fall from the sky. Deception and delusion will be everywhere. Demon-possessed people and reprobates will roam freely and unhindered. People will have no consciences, no natural affection, and no love, only hatred and misery.

The whole world will seemingly be in a deathly dive, plunging rapidly toward some uncertain outcome. The Tribulation will be a time of horror, devastation, and destruction. Property will be confiscated. Friends and family members will betray one another, even bringing death to some. The earth will experience cataclysmic convulsions, natural calamities, famines, and unrest. Food will be scarce. Islands will flee, cities will burn, and volcanoes will erupt with deadly force.

Animals will lose their natural fear of man. Snakes, dogs, deer, spiders, insects, bats, and birds will turn against humans. Demonic beings in the form of tormenting insects will be released from hell. Their sting will be more painful than any pain known to man. People will cry out to die, but death will escape them (Rev. 9:3–6).

As the Antichrist demands worship, he will then use his position to persecute Jews and those who come to Christ after the Rapture. John saw that "it was granted to him to wage war with the saints and to overcome them. And authority was given him over every tribe and tongue and nation" (Rev. 13:7).

Death camps will be established in every region of the world. The preferred method of execution will be beheading. There will be mass executions of Jews and those who openly profess Jesus Christ. That flesh people smell burning in the distance may be coming from the death camp where they just took their sons or daughters. Daniel described it as the shattering of the holy people (Dan. 12:7). The very phrase makes me shudder.

Strangely, during all of these calamities, people will continue to blame Israel for the world's woes. Revelation describes demons like frogs coming out of ambassadors' mouths and spreading lies, convincing them that Israel is the source of all the earth's problems (Rev. 16:13–14). That is what drives the massive extermination campaign. Anyone who tries to protect the Jews will go to the death camps as well. Jesus spoke of this:

> Then they will hand you over to be persecuted and will kill you. And you will be hated by all nations for My name's sake. Then many will fall away, and betray one another, and hate one another. And many false prophets will rise and will deceive many. Because iniquity will abound, the love of many will grow cold.
> —MATTHEW 24:9–12

During this terrible period, those who come to Christ will be able to endure to the end. They will live off the land, stay out of sight, and stay under the radar of the military forces of the world leader. If they get caught, they will give their lives rather than take the mark of loyalty to the world leader, but it's great to know that Jesus promises, "He who endures to the end shall be saved" (Matt. 24:13). I love the word *endure*. It's like a ray of hope in a dark room.

One-half to two-thirds of the world's population will die during the Tribulation. Jesus said except that time be shortened, the whole human race would be wiped out (Matt. 24:22). God will deal with the world severely. Still, His judgments are meant to be redemptive and cause people to cry out to Him while there is still hope.

Unrepentant People

However, many people will not repent. One of the features of the final *shabua* is the lack of repentance in spite of the hammering blows of catastrophes. John observed:

> The rest of mankind, who were not killed by these plagues, did not repent of the works of their hands. They did not cease to worship demons, and idols of gold, silver, brass, stone, and wood, which cannot see nor hear nor walk. Nor did they repent of their murders or their magical arts or their sexual immorality or their thefts.
>
> —Revelation 9:21

> Men were scorched with great heat, and they blasphemed the name of God who has power over these plagues, and they did not repent and give Him glory.... [They] blasphemed the God of heaven because of their pains and their sores, and did not repent of their deeds.
>
> —Revelation 16:9, 11

Let's be clear about what repentance is and is not. It is not merely regretting something or making a confession. It is not simply being sorry. The Bible tells us that godly sorrow brings repentance that leads to salvation and leaves no regret, but worldly sorrow brings death (2 Cor. 7:10).

Repentance is a true reversal. It begins with a recognition that one has sinned, continues with confession, and concludes with changed behavior. Repentance is taking a U-turn and not doing what you did before. Isaiah 55:6 says beautifully, "Seek the LORD while He may be found, call you upon Him while He is near." Hebrews 3:15 agrees, "Today if you will hear His voice, do not harden your hearts, as in the rebellion."

During the final *shabua*, repentance will be in short supply as people cling to their own will despite the obvious manifestation of God's redeeming rebuke.

America Stands By, Helpless

Notice too the absence of America in all of the chaos. During the final *shabua*, the Antichrist will control the media, military, agriculture, health care, economy, global governments, religion, and commerce. Interestingly, and perhaps sadly, America will not be a helpful player. There are a few possible reasons, some of which we discussed in chapter 7.

+ A financial crash may cause America no longer to be a superpower.

+ Our country may be destroyed by nuclear weapons or a military invasion.

+ An electromagnetic pulse may kill our electrical systems—dooming our economy and military.

+ A pestilence may sweep through America as the Spanish flu did a century ago.

+ America may become a part of the European Union as a kind of Western province. After all, we emerged from Europe.

+ Best among the options, perhaps America will experience such great revival that the Rapture will leave the country with far fewer people than it has now.

Although America may not play a role as a great nation, Daniel 11:32 promises, "The people who know their God will be strong and take action." Jesus similarly said, "He who believes in Me will do the works that I do also. And he will do greater works than these" (John 14:12). This is a promise that God will release fresh power on those who take the time to get understanding. These people will do almost unbelievable exploits, things others only dream about.

Russia and Iran Invade

At some point Russia and Iran, along with others, will invade Israel. This could transpire before the Rapture or during the final *shabua*. Ezekiel 38 says Russia will begin to align with Persia, which is modern Iran.

In Ezekiel 38 we read about Israel's end-time invaders: Rosh, Meshek, and Tubal, which were discussed in chapter 6. The army of Russia will go forth with its top ally, Iran, along with several other Muslim nations to take the wealth of Israel. But this invasion will dramatically fail (Ezek. 38:4–6, 22–23). God is going to perform astonishing miracles in the mountains, and five-sixths of the armies are going to die supernaturally. Perhaps their own weapons explode on them, but Israel won't need to lift a finger or fire a single shot. God's got this one.

Ezekiel 39 describes the Russian, Iranian, and other dead bodies piling up and the Jews having to bury them. They will set up flags and not allow people to touch the bodies for some reason. This may mean a chemical or nuclear attack will be made and the bodies or the land will be radioactive. In any case this chapter says the bodies will be buried over the course of seven months, and Israel will use the weapons of warfare for fuel.

The final *shabua*, earth's final years with human government, will last seven years, with the most dreadful part being the final forty-two months. God will not let it go on beyond that. Still, it will seem like an eternity. It will end with the most amazing event in human history—the second coming of Jesus Christ to the earth. But before we examine that glorious and fearsome event, I want to end this chapter with some help for people who may miss the Rapture.

What to Do If You Miss God's Final Roundup—the Rapture

A person can be a professing Christian and not actually be in the faith. Paul said, "Examine yourselves, seeing whether you are in the faith" (2 Cor. 13:5). Jesus said, "Not everyone who says to Me, 'Lord, Lord,' shall enter the kingdom of heaven, but he who does the will of My Father who is in heaven" (Matt. 7:21–23). If you are reading this book after the Rapture has occurred, it's because you weren't ready. Jesus said in Matthew 25:10 that "those who were ready went in.... And the door was shut."

Let me give you twenty pieces of counsel to survive this terrible time if you miss God's first roundup, the Rapture.[6]

Do not believe the explanations given by the secular media.

Christians have not been beamed to some interplanetary spaceship to be reprogrammed. We have not been taken by aliens, and we are not in Buenos Aires, Togo, or Europe. We have left the earth on a cloud of glory to be with Jesus forever.

Get rid of your cell phone.

If you do not agree with the government of the final *shabua* and the charming world leader, you will be hunted. Your cell phone can be tracked. Throw it in a river or lake far from where you are going to be.

Do not kill yourself.

Whenever there is social disorder and confusion, people tend to think that suicide is the only way out. It's not. You probably feel hopeless, but there is still hope. The Holy Spirit will still be working during the final *shabua*. Pray and ask Him to guide you, give you strength, and dwell in you.

Repent immediately and make your peace with God.

If you are reading this after the Rapture, you have already witnessed many of the events I described. Now is the time to repent. Jesus Christ is the only Savior and only way to heaven (John 14:6). Pray, "Lord Jesus, be merciful to me. I have sinned against You. Save me now. I receive You as my personal Savior." For, "Everyone who calls on the name of the Lord shall be saved" (Rom. 10:13).

Make sure you have a printed Bible.

Because digital devices can be tracked, you will not want any electronic tablets during the Tribulation. God's Word and promises will still work after the Rapture, for Jesus said, "Heaven and earth will pass away, but My words will never pass away" (Matt. 24:35). Keep your Bible in a safe place, because when the Antichrist's government takes over, he will eventually try to destroy all the Bibles.

Read the Ten Commandments and follow them (Exod. 20:1–17). God's grace is still available, but after the church is gone, the age of grace has concluded and everything then reverts to something like Old Testament times.

Make sure you read Daniel 2–12. Chapter 12 will give you the general time Jesus is coming the second time. Read Matthew 24; Mark 13; 1 Thessalonians 5; 2 Thessalonians 2; and the Book of Revelation. Everything will begin to make sense to you.

Leave your home and get away from the cities, especially the big cities.

You are going to be tempted to wait and see what happens, but it will be a fatal mistake if you do, just as it was for the Jews who waited too long during the holocaust years. Go to some remote area. Learn to live off the land. Don't take your cell phone, because you can be tracked. Disconnect the transponder on your vehicle, or ditch the vehicle altogether.

Make sure your family is safe and in agreement with your decision to leave. Take them if they will come. If not, you must go alone.

Pray for God to help you and give you strength.

Surviving will be difficult, but God will still hear you, and He will still help you. It won't be easy, but Jesus said, "He who endures to the end shall be saved" (Matt. 24:13). You are going to need His strength like you have never needed it before.

Don't go to church.

That's right—don't go to church or join the world conglomerate religion, because it will be under the control of the False Prophet (Rev. 13). All true, godly ministers will have left the earth in the Rapture. Do not believe the lies of the ministers who are left behind. Even if you see miracles and apparent wonders, do not believe them. They are lying wonders (Matt. 24:24; Mark 13:22; 2 Thess. 2:9). Deception will be the order of the day. Delusion will be everywhere, especially in "churches."

If possible, try to find others who may have accepted Christ after the Rapture. You will be able to find ways to support and encourage one another.

Get a small, self-powered radio.

If you can't get a hand-cranked radio, get a battery-operated radio and a good supply of batteries, because you are going to need to listen. Don't believe the propaganda, but believe reports about certain events relating to wars and geophysical calamities. You will be able to know what will happen next by reading Revelation 6–19.

Keep praying for your loved ones who are unbelievers.

God will still answer prayers during the Tribulation. Your prayers may be the key to seeing your loved ones again after this period of supreme agony is over.

Leave copies of this list (or this book) for as many people as you can.

Perhaps this will help others survive and come to Christ. Be discerning, however, in giving out books like this if the Rapture has already occurred. Jesus said in Luke 21:16–17 that people will be betrayed by parents, brothers, relatives, and friends, and some of them will cause you to be put to death. He was talking about the period you are living in right now if you missed the Rapture.

Do not in any way, under any circumstances, align with the world leader.

Everyone is going to love him and even worship him. But if you listen to his lies, you will be drawn into a strong delusion that will seal your eternal fate (2 Thess. 2:9–12). You will be soon banished to hell because you didn't love the truth.

Refuse to take a mark, a name, a number, or a chip in your body.

Refuse any tattoo or microchip injection, because Revelation 13 says this powerful world leader will require everyone, small and great, rich and poor, free and slave, to be given a mark on their right hand or on their forehead. But once you get it, you will belong to Satan forever. Being shut out of the world economy and losing your physical life is better than being damned forever to the lake of fire (Rev. 14:9–11). The life of many believers during this time of the final *shabua* will end in beheading for refusal to take the mark of the beast (Rev. 20:4).

Do not steal, do not commit any sexual sin, do not murder anyone, and do not use drugs to ease your anxiety.

The temptation to steal, murder, use drugs, and give yourself to sexual sin will be enormous, but you must resist. If you commit these sins, you may find it very difficult to repent (Rev. 9:21).

Pray for the Jewish people and the nation of Israel.

The Jews are going to be suffering to a greater degree than any other group on earth. That is why the final *shabua* is called the Tribulation and the time of Jacob's trouble.

Jesus said this time is going to be worse for the Jewish people than anything they have ever experienced in the past (Matt. 24:21). Psalm 122:6 says, "Pray for the peace of Jerusalem." In Zechariah 14:2 we are told that all the nations of the world will be against Israel in its final holocaust.

Be prepared to suffer.

At some point liquidation camps and facilities will be operating around the clock. As I understand the prophetic warnings of the Great Tribulation, famine will be worse than ever. Families will be separated. Life on earth is going to look like a horror movie, but it's real. You may have to die for your faith, but it will be worth it.

Do not speak evil of Israel or Israel's people, no matter the pressure.

God will contend with you if you are contentious with Israel. False prophets will tell you that the nation of Israel has no right to exist. They will tell you that the people living in Israel are not really Jews and descendants of Abraham. Never speak against Israel or Israel's people (Gen. 12:3; Isa. 49:25).

If you are captured by the authorities, do not deny Jesus Christ as Lord and God.

It is better to die than deny Christ (Luke 12:8–10). In Revelation 6:9–11 we see quite a few people who died after the Rapture for their faith, and they made it to heaven. If you deny Jesus Christ, you will be assigned to Hades (hell's holding tank, so to speak) to await the awful great white throne judgment (Rev. 20:11–12).

Mark the day the world leader moves his image into the holy temple in Jerusalem.

When that happens, you will know that you have 1,260 days to survive. Daniel refers to 1,290 days, which includes 30 days of cleansing after Christ returns.

Determine to endure to the end!

If you miss the Rapture, you can still have hope. Moses endured much tribulation by looking to Him who is invisible (God). Paul wrote, "If we endure, we shall also reign with Him. If we deny Him, He also will deny us" (2 Tim. 2:12).

Chapter 11

THE COMING KINGDOM

AFTER JESUS RETURNS

The kingdoms of the world have become the kingdoms of our
Lord, and of His Christ, and He shall reign forever and ever.
—REVELATION 11:15

T HE WORLD LIES in devastation. Three and a half years of
pummeling and madness have left it scorched and worthless.
More than half of the population has died. Calamities are a daily
occurrence.

Blame for Israel—an insane rage promoted by Satan and vast
hordes of demons let loose on the world—drives the nations to mount
another wave of attacks against Israel. They don't seem to realize that
this final battle, known as Armageddon, also means that human history as we know it is winding down. Everything is about to change
in a moment.

We have been well warned. The Old Testament has more than
1,800 references to the second coming of Christ. The New Testament
refers to His second coming 318 times. This means that one out of
every thirty New Testament verses relates to Christ's return.

And so the nations of the world gather together in a final attempt
to wipe out Israel once and for all. Each nation sends a representative
army. Because of advanced modern weaponry, there aren't as many
people on the battlefield as before. Nevertheless, it will be a fearsome
force—the largest concentration of military power ever gathered in
one place in history.

This battle will happen on a day that is easily predictable.

Remember that from the time the Antichrist moves his image into the temple, there will be 1,260 days until Jesus returns. The battle of Armageddon will begin before that, but on the 1,260th day exactly, the soldiers and generals will look in the sky and see wave after wave of…something. It may appear to be a huge white cloud, a massive flock of birds, or aircraft of some kind. The white cloud will get closer and closer to earth. They will look through their binoculars and scopes and see the Son of God, Jesus, riding a white horse with millions upon millions of followers riding with Him. The biggest posse ever assembled will be coming to save the world. No longer will Jesus be a baby in a manger or a beaten man led to die on a cross. He will come as the Warrior King whose robe is dipped in blood and whose title is emblazoned upon Him: "KING OF KINGS AND LORD OF LORDS."

> I saw heaven opened. And there was a white horse. He who sat on it is called Faithful and True, and in righteousness He judges and wages war. His eyes are like a flame of fire, and on His head are many crowns. He has a name written, that no one knows but He Himself. He is clothed with a robe dipped in blood. His name is called The Word of God. The armies in heaven, clothed in fine linen, white and clean, followed Him on white horses. Out of His mouth proceeds a sharp sword, with which He may strike the nations. "He shall rule them with an iron scepter." He treads the winepress of the fury and wrath of God the Almighty. On His robe and on His thigh He has a name written: KING OF KINGS AND LORD OF LORDS.
>
> —Revelation 19:11–16

Instantly the armies will forget about Israel and turn their weapons toward the risen Son of God! (See Zechariah 14; Revelation 19.) What an amazing deception that they would even think their earthly weapons, no matter how advanced, could have an effect on Him—or us in our glorified bodies! Missiles will zip by but do no harm. Jesus could catch one and throw it back if He wanted, but He won't. Instead, He will simply speak a word that will become like a mighty sword, and the Antichrist, his False Prophet, and all the armies assembled against Israel will crumble (2 Thess. 2:8; Rev. 19:15).

The Real King Is Back

The Lion of the tribe of Judah is back, and He has come to judge the world.

> Look! He is coming with clouds, and every eye will see Him, even those who pierced Him. And all the tribes of the earth will mourn because of Him. Even so, Amen.
> —Revelation 1:7

> Then the sign of the Son of Man will appear in heaven, and then all the tribes of the earth will mourn, and they will see the Son of Man coming on the clouds of heaven with power and great glory.
> —Matthew 24:30

Jesus will then throw the Antichrist and the False Prophet into hell. Everyone who received the mark of loyalty to him will be flung into hell with him (Rev. 14:9–11). They will await the great white throne judgment after the thousand years is complete.

> Then I saw a great white throne and Him who was seated on it. From His face the earth and the heavens fled away, and no place was found for them. And I saw the dead, small and great, standing before God. Books were opened. Then another book was opened, which is the Book of Life. The dead were judged according to their works as recorded in the books.
> —Revelation 20:11–12

Those who did not take the mark of the beast will stay on earth for the millennial reign in their human bodies.

The First Seventy-Five Days

Jesus will step off His steed onto the Mount of Olives, which will split from east to west in a great earthquake (Zech. 14:3–4). He will walk across the Kidron Valley and through the Eastern Gate. There two rabbis with holy anointing oil will pour it over Jesus, anointing Him Messiah forever.

For seventy-five days there will be a cleanup time and judgment.[1] Jesus will judge the nations based on how they treated Israel. During the seventy-five days, there will be great cleanup projects all around the world. All emblems, statues, posters, and murals of the Antichrist will be taken down. Jesus will set up His throne on the throne of David, and Jerusalem will become the capital of the entire world (Ps. 48:1–3; Hosea 3:5).

Jesus and His team will begin to organize earth's governments, and we will work with Him in our appointed millennial assignments. We will be commissioned to be mayors, city council members, governors, business leaders, and so on. Christ followers will hold all positions of authority on the earth.

Those Who Survive the Final *Shabua*

What about the people who survive the Tribulation? They will continue to live on the earth. They will remain human beings without glorified bodies. But they will be supremely blessed under their new Ruler. Longevity will greatly increase. People will live to be four hundred or five hundred years old. If somebody dies at age one hundred, people will shake their heads and say, "He was so young."

> No longer will babies die when only a few days old. No longer will adults die before they have lived a full life. No longer will people be considered old at one hundred! Only the cursed will die that young!
>
> —ISAIAH 65:20, NLT

People will have natural children and grandchildren. They will still be capable of sin, which is why the Bible says that Jesus and His followers will govern with a rod of iron.

The Millennium is going to be a golden age but not a perfect age. Sickness and evil will be greatly diminished. Jesus will show the world for one thousand years what it would have been like if we had followed God's plan in the first place instead of being drawn away by doubt and self-will. True peace and prosperity will flourish.

God's glory will light up the city (Isa. 4:4–6). Right living will be enforced (Rev. 2:26–27). There will be no more severe storms. The climate will be just right for wonderful agriculture (Isa. 30:23–24). Animals will live at peace with one another and will not pose a threat to humans.

> The wolf also shall dwell with the lamb, and the leopard shall lie down with the young goat, and the calf and the young lion and the fatling together; and a little child shall lead them. The cow and the bear shall graze; their young ones shall lie down together; and the lion shall eat straw like the ox. The nursing child shall play by the hole of the asp, and the weaned child shall put his hand in the viper's den.
>
> —Isaiah 11:6–8

Satan will be absent, and we will turn weapons of war into implements of productivity: "They will beat their swords into plowshares, and their spears into pruning hooks. Nation will not take up sword against nation, and they will no longer train for war" (Mic. 4:3). There will be no more wars or rumors of war. Jerusalem, known for thousands of years for war, bloodshed, and global distress, will at last become the city of peace. God will keep His promise to Mary that Jesus will rule from David's throne:

> He will be great, and will be called the Son of the Highest. And the Lord God will give Him the throne of His father

David, and He will reign over the house of Jacob forever. And of His kingdom there will be no end.

—Luke 1:32–33

People will love visiting Jerusalem and learning more about God.

The mountain of the Lord's house shall be established on the top of the mountains, and shall be exalted above the hills, and all nations shall flow to it. Many people shall go and say, "Come, and let us go up to the mountain of the Lord, to the house of the God of Jacob, and He will teach us of His ways, and we will walk in His paths."

—Isaiah 2:2–3

Jews have feared the name of Jesus for centuries. During the thousand-year reign of Christ on earth, Jewish people will love the name of Jesus and will say with the prophet of old, "For unto us a child is born, unto us a son is given, and the government shall be upon his shoulder. And his name shall be called Wonderful Counselor, Mighty God, Eternal Father, Prince of Peace" (Isa. 9:6).

There will be no such thing as adversarial government where people vie for the same position, debating and advertising why they are better. There will be no elections and no candidates. Jesus will personally appoint leaders in His kingdom based on their faithfulness during their lives on earth. True justice will prevail.

Many peoples and strong nations will seek out the Lord of Hosts in Jerusalem and to entreat the favor of the Lord. Thus says the Lord of Hosts: In those days ten men from every language of the nations will take hold of the garment of a Jew, saying, "Let us go with you, for we have heard that God is with you."

—Zechariah 8:22–23

The Millennium will be known as the kingdom age. Technically we are in the kingdom age now in that we can function on its principles and laws and expand its scope with our prayers and actions. We are in the spiritual phase of the kingdom, but during the Millennium we will see the physical kingdom birthed on earth, with Jesus Christ as the true world leader. What a huge relief after what happened in the final *shabua*! A universal knowledge of the Lord will exist (Isa. 11:9; Zech. 8:22–23), and there will be no need for evangelism as we know it today. Sin will never be remembered.

> They shall teach no more every man his neighbor and every man his brother, saying, "Know the LORD," for they all shall know Me, from the least of them to the greatest of them, says the LORD, for I will forgive their iniquity, and I will remember their sin no more.
>
> —JEREMIAH 31:34

We are headed for a thousand years of real peace and great abundance.

The End of the Millennium

At the end of the thousand years, Satan will be loosed for a short season because every human must be tested by being given a choice to reject God. Those of us who have come back to earth with Christ— those who went in the Rapture of the church—are not going to be tempted by evil anymore. We already have received our glorified bodies. But many offspring will be born to those who survive the Tribulation. Some of them will choose Satan's way and attempt an invasion of Israel to overthrow Jesus (Rev. 20:7–15).

The rebellion will be squelched, and those who support it will be immediately cast into hell. Then the second resurrection will take place. Spirits in Hades will be reunited with their bodies and be given bodies that can still feel, have emotions, and hunger and thirst but never die. They will be caught up before the great white throne, and every one of them will be declared guilty. This is the judgment for those whose names are not written in the Book of Life. The small, the great, the rich, the poor, the hideous evil leaders of history, and the so-called good, moral people who simply never accepted Jesus Christ—each of them had an opportunity to love God and respond to His call but did not. Everyone had an opportunity to freely come to God on His terms, but instead they chose against Christ. They chose sin over righteousness. They chose something else over God's Son. Because their names are not written in the Book of Life, they will hear the words, "I do not know you....Depart from Me, all you workers of iniquity. I don't know you" (Luke 13:27).

There will be weeping, wailing, and gnashing of teeth (Matt. 25:30). And God will assign these poor souls to the lake of fire, the garbage dump of all creation. Filth, demons, and the devil himself will be there. Souls will be tormented there forever. There will be no way out. No prayer will ever be heard from its residents. It's too late. For those with Christ, God will remove the memory of those people as if they never existed.

The Earth Is Recommissioned

What happens next is amazing. The earth is going to be burned—not to destroy it but to cleanse it. The world will not end but will be washed by fire from all the sin that was acted out on this planet. Earth will be recommissioned and resurrected. There will be a new earth with a new view of the heavens, and we are told in Revelation that a cube-shaped city called New Jerusalem, approximately 1,400 miles in length, breadth, and height, will come down from heaven and land on earth (Rev. 21:1–4, 16).

We will have perfect access to the earth, New Jerusalem, and heaven, God's place of abode. We will have mansions in heaven, business in the New Jerusalem, and activities on the earth anytime we want. Everything will glorify Jesus. There will be activity, business, places to go, meaningful service, fun things to do, and people to be with.

The best is yet to come. The Bible describes it this way: "The kingdoms of the world have become the kingdoms of our Lord, and of His Christ, and He shall reign forever and ever" (Rev. 11:15).

Jesus will hand over ownership of the earth to His Father, and we will continue into eternity with Him. It's almost too incredible to fathom, but I know one thing: I can't wait to experience it. How about you?

Chapter 12

FINAL WORDS

ADMONITIONS AND ENCOURAGEMENT

Dear brothers and sisters, I close my letter with these last words: Be joyful. Grow to maturity. Encourage each other. Live in harmony and peace. Then the God of love and peace will be with you.

—2 CORINTHIANS 13:11, NLT

A s you can see, all the borders of the prophetic puzzle are now in place. Nearly every day other pieces are falling into their proper positions, signaling that the Day of the Lord is rapidly approaching.

Peter warned of those who would mock those who speak of Christ's second coming: "Know this first, that there shall come scoffers in the last days who walk after their own lusts" (2 Pet. 3:3–4). I find many of these scoffers, unfortunately, in the professing church!

Defectors From the Faith

The apostle Paul forecasted a time of apostasy prior to Christ's coming. This apostasy would actually be the final action that would give rise to the satanic world leader.

> Let no one in any way deceive or entrap you, for that day will not come unless the apostasy comes first [that is, the great rebellion, the abandonment of the faith by professed Christians], and the man of lawlessness is revealed, the son of destruction [the Antichrist, the one who is destined to be destroyed].
>
> —2 THESSALONIANS 2:3, AMP

Defection from the faith unfortunately will increase. Jesus warned that the first sign of His return would be deception (Matt. 24:4, 23). Deception leads to delusion. Delusion leads to apostasy and ultimately an abandonment of the fundamentals of Christianity. It was Israel's apostasy throughout history that brought God's judgment. Judgment begins in the house of God.

The influence of the church on our nation and the world depends on solid Bible preaching and teaching from our pulpits and on God's people reaching out to their loved ones and neighbors with the gospel of Jesus Christ and the good news of His kingdom.

Some professing Christians today cry, "I'm not interested in doctrine; I'm only interested in unity." But unity with false doctrines and systems has never brought true revival. In the past, *ecumenicalism* was defined as "unity among various Christian denominations in an effort to find common ground with other believers." Today it is taking on another meaning that now includes other religions.

Pope Francis redefined the word *ecumenical* when, in an unprecedented move, he invited Muslims to pray at the Vatican.[1] Unity among believers is admirable, but unity with the theologically aberrant is unacceptable for godly followers of Jesus. Instead, we must point out and expose works of darkness (Eph. 5:11). Eternity is at stake here. Some undiscerning church members, to their own peril, stay in churches that have gone sideways doctrinally because their parents or their grandparents went to the church or perhaps because they have given a lot of money to past building programs and feel tied to the church.

The First Three Things I Look for in a Church

There are many factors that make a great church. But the top three are the pastor, the doctrines, and the worship of God.

Where did the pastor get his or her credentials?

Did the pastor receive his license to preach or ordination from a recognized credentialing body? Did the pastor get credentials online at some Internet organization that most have never heard about?

In years gone by, you could find advertisements in tabloids (the kind sold in the checkout lane at grocery stores) offering ordination for those who wanted to become a minister. In fact, a friend of mine actually had his cat and dog ordained for ten dollars each from one of these bogus credentialing agencies. Make sure the pastor is qualified, both doctrinally and morally, before selecting a church.

What are the doctrines of the church?

Do they believe in salvation by God's grace through faith in Christ's finished work? Do they believe the Bible is God's inerrant, infallible Word? Do they take the Bible literally? Are any of the fundamental doctrines of the faith negotiable in this church? For example, do they solidly teach the virgin birth of Jesus Christ and that He was conceived of the Holy Spirit? Do they believe that Jesus died on the cross for the sin of the world and rose again the third day? What do they believe about eschatology? Are they amillennial, postmillennial, or premillennial? Is the church pro-Israel? Is the church concerned about the lost and involved in evangelism and making disciples?

Does the church encourage the worship of God?

True worship of God involves the heart (spiritual), the head (attitudinal), and the hand (practical). These three elements are present not only in the singing portion of a Sunday service but in all of life. You see, worship is much more than the songs we sing or the corporate expression we give to it. Worship is an all-encompassing lifestyle.

If we understand true worship, we know that people shouldn't start worshipping when they come into a church service—they should continue worshipping! We bring our worshipping lifestyles with us into a corporate setting, and when we leave, we continue worshipping beyond the walls of the church building.

Jesus gave the definition of *worship* when He said, "Yet the hour is coming, and is now here, when the true worshippers will worship the Father in spirit and truth. For the Father seeks such to worship Him. God is Spirit, and those who worship Him must worship Him in spirit and truth" (John 4:23–24).

"Spirit and truth" worship, which the Father seeks, means a life of integrity, sincerity, honesty and dedication. Every church and its leadership should encourage whole-life worship as Paul described in one of his letters:

> I urge you therefore, brothers, by the mercies of God, that you present your bodies as a living sacrifice, holy, and acceptable to God, which is your reasonable service of worship. Do not be conformed to this world, but be transformed by the renewing of your mind, that you may prove what is the good and acceptable and perfect will of God.
>
> —ROMANS 12:1–2

Are the people of the church worshipping beyond the walls? Are they being motivated to minister in practical ways in the community, thus proving "what is the good and acceptable and perfect will of God"? Are they worshipping alone in their homes and in small group meetings? That is a healthy church and a true lifestyle of worship.

One of the many benefits of a worshipping lifestyle is that it relieves Sunday mornings of the pressure to fulfill everyone's musical expectations. Each church has its own style of music, whether the songs are sung from an old hymnbook or the worship team uses more contemporary methods and music. Style is really not the point. God likes the diversity of approaches different churches take.

My wife and I went to California where I was to speak at a church we had never been to. We didn't know what to expect that morning, and the style of music really surprised us. It was sort of a country-Latino mix. We had never heard such a style in church before, but both my wife and I were lifted into an unusual presence of God and felt like Jesus was right there in the auditorium. Later we learned that every musician and singer had invested hours in prayer before the service. "Worship time" wasn't a show or a performance; it was ongoing ministry to Jesus Himself.

Leading a worship service or preaching God's Word is a sincere time of honoring God and giving Jesus preeminence. We shouldn't so much ask ourselves, "Do I really like this church's style of music?" but rather, "Does this body of believers give Jesus Christ preeminence in everything? Is Jesus glorified in the music, the preaching, and other ministries in the church?" If so, hop on board and worship with all you have!

Other matters that are important include children's and youth ministries, biblical training, lay involvement, fellowship, prayer, good preaching and teaching, and music, but foremost are an honorable pastor, pure doctrine, and true worship.

Defend Against Deception

Corrupt theology today travels at lightning speed because of the Internet. It then quickly makes its way into our pulpits, seminaries, and schools. Again, it was Jesus who said, "Not everyone who says to Me, 'Lord, Lord,' shall enter the kingdom of heaven, but he who does the will of My Father who is in heaven" (Matt. 7:21).

The nature of deception is that you think you're right when you're wrong.

I acquired a book about the most evil dictators of all time and discovered that 99 percent of the evil done in the world is carried out by deluded people who are convinced they are absolutely right and believe they are right all of the time. They give no thought to nor repent of the evil they perpetrated because they are right, at least in their own minds.[2]

Jesus said, "Beware of false prophets who come to you in sheep's clothing, but inwardly they are ravenous wolves" (Matt. 7:15). The good news is this: when we stay connected to Jesus Christ, His Spirit, and His Word, we will develop supernatural discernment and find true hope in these last days (Ps. 119:49; Col. 1:5; Heb. 5:14).

Discernment is our divine defense against deception, delusion, and apostasy.

The question is this: Is there really any hope? Yes, but only in Jesus Christ. God promised a blessed hope for those who walk with Him as Enoch did.

> We await the blessed hope and the appearing of the glory of our great God and Savior Jesus Christ.
>
> —TITUS 2:13

> By faith Enoch was taken to heaven so that he would not see death. He was not found, because God took him away. For before he was taken, he had this commendation, that he pleased God.
>
> —HEBREWS 11:5

Jesus is coming for His bride, the church, in the twinkling of an eye. We shall meet Him in the clouds. That is a great hope.

In these last days some will arise who will possess great understanding of the times and will perform miracles in the name of Christ. You can be one of these amazing last days giants in the faith.

Preparing for the Final Hours

How do you prepare?

First, prepare spiritually. Know the Lord personally and intimately and walk with Him daily. Intercede for others. Make sure your family knows Jesus.

Second, prepare attitudinally. Be at peace in Christ; trust Him implicitly. Even in the worst times imaginable, He encouraged, "Let not your heart be troubled" (John 14:27). I know it can be scary, but God hasn't given us a spirit of fear.

Third, prepare practically. This is where you take action steps, putting on the armor of God daily and doing something every day to help others in their journeys of faith. Fellowship with like-minded believers.

But the people who know their God will be strong and take action.

                                              —Daniel 11:32

Thank you for joining me on this journey into *Hope in the Last Days*.

HOW TO ASK JESUS TO BE YOUR SAVIOR AND BECOME A PART OF HIS KINGDOM

Admit you have sinned and offended God.

I didn't realize until November of 1971 that even one sin can keep a person from heaven unless he has the Savior. Have you ever gossiped or lied? You've sinned. Have you ever dishonored your parents? You've sinned. Have you ever lusted? Have you ever hated another person? You've sinned.

> For all have sinned and come short of the glory of God.
> —ROMANS 3:23

Accept the gift of life God offers you.

It's found through Jesus Christ, who took the punishment for you by carrying your sins on the cross.

> For the wages of sin is death, but the gift of God is eternal life through Jesus Christ our Lord.
> —ROMANS 6:23

Receive Jesus as your only hope of ever having a home in heaven and a role in His kingdom.

> Yet to all who received Him, He gave the power to become sons of God, to those who believed in His name.
> —JOHN 1:12

Pray this prayer, and God will hear and forgive you, give you a new nature, and prepare a home in heaven for you.

Father in Heaven, I come to You in the name of Your Son, Jesus. I have sinned against You. Please forgive me and cleanse me. I believe Jesus died on the cross for me, and I believe He was raised from the dead and lives forevermore. Jesus, come into my heart and life. Be my Savior, my Lord, and my best friend. I trust You to give me a home in heaven and a new start in life beginning now. Amen!

If you prayed that prayer, I'd love to give you a free download of my book, *The New Life—The Start of Something Wonderful.* You can download a copy by visiting www.DaveWilliams.com/FreeNewLife.

NOTES

Introduction

1. Isaac Newton, as quoted in Charles Eisenberg, *The Book of Daniel—A Well Kept Secret* (Maitland, FL: Xulon Press 2007), 32.

Chapter 1
History Converges: The Times and the Seasons

1. Chuck Missler, "How Will the World Explain the Rapture?," April 9, 2013, accessed March 3, 2016, http://www.khouse.org/enews_article /2013/2068/; Remnant Report.com, accessed November 16, 2016, http:// remnantreport.com/cgi-bin/imcart/read.cgi?article_id=146&sub=4/.

2. Michael Morris, "Mark Levin: 'World War III Has Begun,'" CNSNews.com, September 25, 2014, accessed October 27, 2016, http:// www.cnsnews.com/mrctv-blog/michael-morris/mark-levin-world-war-iii -has-begun.

3. Marshall Connolly, "Pope Francis: World War III Has Begun—Third Secret of Fatima Gives Warning," Catholic Online, November 19, 2015, accessed October 27, 2016, http://www.catholic.org/news/hf/faith /story.php?id=65403.

4. Ari Yashar, "Russia Is Giving Hezbollah Advanced Weapons," Arutz Sheva, November 1, 2016, accessed January 2, 2017, http://www .israelnationalnews.com/News/News.aspx/206270.

5. "Report: Hezbollah Prepares for 'Biggest War Ever' with Israel," Ynet, originally published March 4, 2016, updated April 3, 2016, accessed October 27, 2016, http://www.ynetnews.com/articles/0,7340,L-4774325,00 .html.

6. Shepard Smith, Fox News, November 13, 2015.

7. Richard Abanes, *End-Time Visions: The Road to Armageddon* (New York: Four Walls Eight Windows, 1998), 95–96.

8. Dan Amira, "A Conversation With Harold Camping, Prophesier of Judgment Day," *New York*, May 11, 2011, accessed October 28, 2016, http:// nymag.com/daily/intelligencer/2011/05/a_conversation_with_harold_cam .html.

9. Luiza Oleszczuk, "Harold Camping Exclusive: Family Radio Founder Retires; Doomsday 'Prophet' No Longer Able to Work," *Christian Post*, October 24, 2011, accessed January 2, 2017, http://www.christianpost.com/news/harold-camping-exclusive-family-radio-founder-retires-doomsday-prophet-no-longer-able-to-work-59222/.

10. Edgar Whisenant, *88 Reasons Why the Rapture Could Be in 1988* (Nashville: World Bible Society, 1988); Edgar Whisenant, *On Borrowed Time* (Nashville: World Bible Society, 1988).

11. Hank Hanegraaff, "John Hinkle-D-Day Declarations," *Christian Research Journal*, Fall 1995, accessed October 28, 2016, http://www.equip.org/article/john-hinkle-d-day-declarations.

12. "Church Planting Movements: How Fast Do They Grow?," *Disciple All Nations* (blog), February 21, 2014, accessed October 28, 2016, https://discipleallnations.wordpress.com/tag/cuba/.

13. "Muslims Turning to Christ—a Global Phenomenon," accessed November 7, 2016, https://www.premierchristianity.com/Past-Issues/2016/June-2016/Muslims-turning-to-Christ-a-global-phenomenon/; "Millions of Muslims Converting to Christianity," July 29, 2014, accessed November 9, 2016, http://www.crosswalk.com/blogs/christian-trends/millions-of-muslims-converting-to-christ.html/.

14. "Evangelists Say Muslims Coming to Christ at Historic Rate," August 20, 2010, accessed January 1, 2017, http://www.charismamag.com/site-archives/570-news/featured-news/11719-evangelists-say-muslims-coming-to-christ-at-historic-rate.

15. J. D. King, "The Underground Revival in the Middle East That Might Take Down Islam," Charisma News, November 25, 2015, accessed October 28, 2016, http://www.charismanews.com/opinion/53443-the-underground-revival-in-the-middle-east-that-might-take-down-islam.

16. Steve Strang, "Can This Be True? 2 Million Indonesian Muslims Find Jesus Per Year," Charisma News, April 7, 2015, accessed October 28, 2016, http://www.charismanews.com/opinion/49079-can-this-be-true-2-million-indonesian-muslims-find-jesus-per-year.

17. J. D. King, "The Underground Revival in the Middle East That Might Take Down Islam," Charisma News, November 25, 2015, accessed October 28, 2016, http://www.charismanews.com/opinion/53443-the-underground-revival-in-the-middle-east-that-might-take-down-islam.

18. "The Top 20 Countries Where Christianity Is Growing the Fastest," *Disciple All Nations* (blog), August 25, 2013, accessed October 28, 2016, https://discipleallnations.wordpress.com/2013/08/25/the-top-20-countries-where-christianity-is-growing-the-fastest/.

19. Ed Hindson, *Final Signs* (Eugene, OR: Harvest House, 1996).

Chapter 2
Avoiding Prohetic Pitfalls and Defining Eschatological Terms

1. Frank Boyd, *Prophetic Light* (Springfield, MO: Gospel Publishing House, 1968).

2. "Biblical Prophecies Fulfilled by Jesus," CBN, accessed January 1, 2017, http://www1.cbn.com/biblestudy/biblical-prophecies-fulfilled-by -jesus.

3. Walter Martin, "Cult of Liberal Theology," 1987, https://www .youtube.com/watch?v=tSDvu3NWBnI, transcribed in "Dr. Walter Martin Speaking Out on Wolves & Cults," ChurchWatch Central, February 7, 2016, accessed October 28, 2016, https://churchwatchcentral.com /2016/02/07/dr-walter-martin-speaking-out-on-wolves-cults/.

4. Blue Letter Bible, s.v. "*elpis*," accessed October 28, 2016, https:// www.blueletterbible.org/lang/lexicon/lexicon.cfm?Strongs=G1680&t =KJV.

5. Based on the author's recollection.

6. Based on the author's recollection.

7. Based on the author's recollection.

8. Ron Rhodes, as quoted in Jonathan Petersen, "8 Great Debates of Bible Prophecy: An Interview with Ron Rhodes," *BibleGateway Blog*, September 12, 2014, accessed October 28, 2016, https://www.biblegateway.com /blog/2014/09/8-great-debates-of-bible-prophecy-an-interview-with-ron -rhodes/.

9. Ron Rhodes, "Rightly Interpreting the Bible," Reasoning from the Scriptures Ministries, accessed October 31, 2016, http://home.earthlink .net/~ronrhodes/Interpretation.html.

Chapter 3
The Spirit of Prophecy: How I Personally Met Jesus in Bible Prophecy

1. Apostles' Creed.

Chapter 4
The Prophetic Chronology: Nothing Makes Sense Without This

1. Stoyan Zaimov, "Billy Graham Says His Heart Aches for 'Deceived' America," *Christian Post*, July 26, 2012, accessed October 31, 2016, http:// www.christianpost.com/news/billy-graham-says-his-heart-aches-for-sinful -deceived-america-78949/.

2. Juliet Eilperin, "For Obama, Rainbow White House Was 'a Moment Worth Savoring,'" *Washington Post*, June 30, 2015, accessed October 31, 2016, https://www.washingtonpost.com/news/post-politics/wp/2015/06/30 /for-obama-rainbow-white-house-was-a-moment-worth-savoring/.

3. Bethany Blankley, "Planned Parenthood's Goddess Projected Onto Empire State Building," Charisma News, August 20, 2015, accessed October 31, 2016, http://www.charismanews.com/opinion/51132-planned -parenthood-s-goddess-projected-onto-empire-state-building.

4. Polly Mosendz, "After Video Accuses Planned Parenthood of 'Selling Body Parts,' Bobby Jindal Announces Investigation," *Newsweek*, July 14, 2015, accessed January 12, 2017, http://www.newsweek.com/after -video-accuses-planned-parenthood-selling-body-parts-bobby-jindal-353828.

5. "Oregon Bakery Owners Refuse to Pay Damages in Gay Wedding Cake Case," Fox News, October 1, 2015, accessed October 31, 2016, http:// www.foxnews.com/us/2015/10/01/oregon-bakery-owners-refuse-to-pay -damages-in-gay-wedding-cake-case.html.

6. "Kentucky Clerk Kim Davis Released From Jail," CBS News, September 8, 2015, accessed October 31, 2016, http://www.cbsnews.com/news /kentucky-clerk-kim-davis-released-from-jail/.

7. Edward Denny, as quoted in Theodore H. Epp et al., *A Brief Outline of Things to Come: The Great Commission: A Vindication and an Interpretation* (n.p.: Solid Christian Books 2015), 16.

8. See *Blue Letter Bible*, s.v. "*mystērion*," accessed January 12, 2017, https://www.blueletterbible.org/lang/lexicon/lexicon.cfm?Strongs =G3466&t=KJV.

9. "Rise of Anti-Semitism in Europe 'Major Threat,' Say Jewish Leaders," RT, March 3, 2016, accessed November 10, 2016, https://www .rt.com/news/334422-european-jews-anti-semitism/.

10. Donna Rachel Edmunds, "Anti-Semitism on the Rise: European Terror Attacks Fuel Hate Crimes Against Jews," Breitbart, July 30, 2015, accessed October 31, 2016, http://www.breitbart.com/london/2015/07/30 /anti-semitism-on-the-rise-european-terror-attacks-fuel-hate-crimes-against -jews/.

11. Jack Van Impe, "A Message of Hope From Dr. Jack Van Impe," Jack Van Impe Ministries International, May 18, 2015, accessed October 31, 2016, http://www.jvim.com/may-18-2015/.

12. pjmiller (username), "The Catastrophic Fall of Jerusalem in 70 A.D.," *Sola Dei Gloria* (blog), March 30, 2008, accessed October 31, 2016, https:// pjmiller.wordpress.com/2008/03/30/the-catastrophic-fall-of-jerusalem-in -70-ad/.

13. Lyric Duveyoung, "What Percentage of the World's Jews Died During WW2?" Quora, November 19, 2013, accessed December 20, 2016, https://www.quora.com/What-percentage-of-the-worlds-Jews-died-during -WW2.

Chapter 5
Preview Signs of the Apocalypse: A Sneak Peek Into the Future

1. "After Gay Marriage Decision: Surprise Blood Moon Displays in Sky Only Over America," Jews News, July 6, 2015, accessed December 20, 2016, http://www.jewsnews.co.il/2015/07/06/after-gay-marriage-decision -surprise-blood-moon-displays-in-sky-only-over-america.html.

2. Barry Secrest, "Signs: Historic 'Star of Bethlehem' Reappears for First Time in Over 2,000 Years, Tonight," Conservative Focus, June 30, 2015, accessed December 20, 2016, http://conservativerefocus.com/blogs /index.php/Religion/signs-historic-star-of-bethlehem; Michael Pearson, "'Double Star' Moment for Jupiter and Venus in the Night Sky," CNN, June 30, 2015, updated July 1, 2015, accessed December 20, 2016, http:// www.cnn.com/2015/06/30/us/feat-jupiter-venus-conjunction.

3. Greg Botelho, "Water Crisis in Flint, Michigan, Draws Federal Investigation," CNN, January 9, 2016, accessed November 1, 2016, http:// www.cnn.com/2016/01/05/health/flint-michigan-water-investigation/; "Flint Water Crisis Fast Facts," CNN, October 17, 2016, updated December 21, 2016, accessed January 1, 2017, http://www.cnn.com/2016/03 /04/us/flint-water-crisis-fast-facts/.

4. Andrew Keller, "United Way Estimates Cost of Helping Children $100M," WNEM, January 18, 2016, updated January 19, 2016, accessed November 1, 2016, http://www.wnem.com/story/30995770/united-way -estimates-cost-of-helping-children-100m.

5. Khalil AlHajal, "87 Cases, 10 Fatal, of Legionella Bacteria Found in Flint Area; Connection to Water Crisis Unclear," MLive, January 13, 2016, updated January 14, 2016, accessed November 1, 2016, http://www.mlive .com/news/detroit/index.ssf/2016/01/legionaires_disease_spike_disc.html.

6. Ambika Vishwanath, "The Water Wars Waged by Islamic State," *Forbes*, November 25, 2015, accessed November 1, 2016, http://www.forbes .com/sites/stratfor/2015/11/25/the-water-wars-waged-by-the-islamic-state /#67166f21733f.

7. Erin Cunningham, "Islamic State Jihadists Are Using Water as a Weapon in Iraq," *Washington Post*, October 7, 2014, accessed November 1, 2016, https://www.washingtonpost.com/world/middle_east/islamic-state -jihadists-are-using-water-as-a-weapon-in-iraq/2014/10/06/aead6792-79 ec-4c7c-8f2f-fd7b95765d09_story.html.

8. "Euphrates River Drying Up Prophesied," Hope of Israel Baptist Mission, February 21, 2015, accessed November 1, 2016, http://hopeof israel.net/news/euphrates-river-drying-prophesied/.

9. "'You Voted Trump' Yelled at Man While He's Beaten in Chicago Streets," CBS, November 11, 2016, updated November 12, 2016, accessed

December 20, 2016, http://www.cbsnews.com/news/you-voted-donald
-trump-yelled-man-beaten-chicago-streets/.

10. Leonardo Blair, "Heartbreaking: Egyptian Christians Were Calling
for Jesus During Execution by ISIS in Libya," February 18, 2015, accessed
December 20, 2016, http://www.christianpost.com/news/heartbreaking
-egyptian-christians-were-calling-for-jesus-during-execution-by-isis-in
-libya-134340/.

11. Jared Malsin, "Christians Mourn Their Relatives Beheaded by ISIS,"
Time, February 23, 2015, accessed December 20, 2016, http://time.com
/3718470/isis-copts-egypt.

12. Ishaan Tharoor, "A Year Ago, ISIS Burned a Jordanian Pilot to
Death. His Family Is Still Anguished," *Washington Post*, February 4, 2016,
accessed December 20, 2016, https://www.washingtonpost.com/news
/worldviews/wp/2016/02/04/a-year-ago-isis-burned-a-jordanian-pilot-to
-death-his-family-is-still-anguished.

13. Mark Berman, "Violent Crime and Murders Both Went Up in 2015,
FBI Says," *Washington Post*, September 26, 2016, accessed December 20,
2016, https://www.washingtonpost.com/news/post-nation/wp/2016/09/26
/violent-crime-and-murders-both-went-up-in-2015-fbi-says/?utm_term
=.dd4db984e482.

14. Analise Ortiz, "Victim of Identity Theft Racks Up Five Criminal
Convictions," ValleyCentral.com, November 17, 2016, accessed December
20, 2016, http://valleycentral.com/news/local/victim-of-identity-theft
-racks-up-five-criminal-convictions.

15. Linda Carroll, "Worldwide Surge in 'Great' Earthquakes Seen in
Past 10 Years," NBC News, October 25, 2014, accessed December 20, 2016,
http://www.nbcnews.com/science/science-news/worldwide-surge-great
-earthquakes-seen-past-10-years-n233661.

16. "Today's Biggest Earthquakes," Earthquake Track, accessed January
12, 2017, http://earthquaketrack.com/.

17. Katharine Lackey, "The World's Deadliest Earthquakes in Past
Decade," *USA Today*, September 16, 2015, accessed December 20, 2016,
http://www.usatoday.com/story/news/world/2015/04/25/worlds-deadliest
-earthquake/26357241.

18. "Pestilences—A Sign," Bibleline Ministries, accessed December 20,
2016, http://www.biblelineministries.org/articles/basearch.php3?action
=full&mainkey=PESTILENCES+-+A+SIGN.

19. "Outbreaks Chronology: Ebola Virus Disease," Centers for Disease
Control and Prevention, accessed December 20, 2016, http://www.cdc.gov
/vhf/ebola/outbreaks/history/chronology.html.

20. Ariana Eunjung Cha, "The Ebola Outbreak May Have Been Bigger Than Believed, With 'Invisible' Infection," *Washington Post*, November 17, 2016, accessed December 20, 2016, https://www.washingtonpost.com/news /to-your-health/wp/201/11/17/the-ebola-outbreak-may-have-been-bigger -than-believed-with-invisible-infection/?utm_term=.1e4458e67154.

21. "Zika Virus," Centers for Disease Control and Prevention, accessed January 12, 2017, https://www.cdc.gov/zika/healtheffects/birth_defects .html.

22. "Department of Health Daily Zika Update," Florida Health, December 19, 2016, accessed December 20, 2016, http://www.floridahealth .gov/newsroom/2016/11/111616-zika-update.html.

23. "Syria: The Story of the Conflict," BBC, March 11, 2016, accessed December 20, 2016, http://www.bbc.com/news/world-middle-east-26116868.

24. "The Guardian View on Turkey: Beware an Elected Dictatorship," *Guardian*, July 17, 2016, accessed December 20, 2016, https://www .theguardian.com/commentisfree/2016/jul/17/the-guardian-view-on -turkey-beware-an-elected-dictatorship.

25. Kyle Cheney, "The 12 Biggest Moments of the GOP Debate," Politico, January 14, 2016, accessed November 1, 2016, http://www.politico .com/story/2016/01/the-5-biggest-moments-of-the-gop-debate-217773.

26. "North Korea Threatens War with U.S. in Propaganda Film," CNN, March 28, 2016, accessed November 1, 2016, http://www.cnn.com /videos/world/2016/03/29/north-korea-propaganda-video-nuclear-war -paula-hancocks-lkl.cnn/video/playlists/north-korea-tensions/.

27. Franklin Graham's Facebook page, March 17, 2015, accessed November 1, 2016, https://www.facebook.com/FranklinGraham/posts /886848164704699.

28. *Oxford Dictionary*, s.v. *"aporia,"* accessed December 20, 2016, https:// en.oxforddictionaries.com/definition/aporia.

29. "Global Debt Enters Terminal Velocity Mode: Why Central Banks Have No Intention of Slowing Their Public and Private Debt Binge," My Budget 360, accessed December 20, 2016, http://www.mybudget360.com /global-debt-total-central-bank-balance-sheet-expansion-debt/.

30. Jonathan Mark, "Evangelicals at the Crossroads," *Good News in the Public Square* (blog), February 20, 2014, accessed November 2, 2016, http:// www.pastorjoelhunter.com/blog/1223; Ronald L. Ray, "Christian Evangelicals Turning Backs on Israel," American Free Press, accessed November 2, 2016, https://americanfreepress.net/christian-evangelicals-turning-backs -on-israel/?print=print.

31. James Delingpole, "People Who Say Climate Change Is Worse Than Terrorism Are Dangerous Liars," Breitbart, November 17, 2015, accessed

December 20, 2016, http://www.breitbart.com/big-government/2015/11/17
/people-say-climate-change-worse-terrorism-dangerous-liars/.

Chapter 6
Last Days Nations and Groups: The Chilling Accuracy of the Ancient Prophets

1. James Slack, "Plans Have Been Drawn Up for a Full-Blown 'United
States of Europe' and Britain Will Have Little Say, Warns Top Tory Minister," *Daily Mail*, April 24, 2016, accessed November 2, 2016, http://www
.dailymail.co.uk/news/article-3556298/Plans-drawn-blown-United-States
-Europe-Britain-little-say-warns-Tory-minister.html; Nick Gutteridge,
"United States of Europe in just 9 Months! The Juncker Plan Revealed in
12-Month EU Roadmap," *Express*, September 16, 2016, accessed November
2, 2016, http://www.express.co.uk/news/politics/711387/European-Union
-Juncker-plan-economy-army-Brussels-led-superstate.

2. "Graphics Guide to the European Emblem," European Union,
accessed November 2, 2016, http://publications.europa.eu/code/en/en
-5000100.htm.

3. "Europe," wildolive, accessed November 2, 2016, http://www
.wildolive.co.uk/europe.htm.

4. European Youth Portal, accessed December 20, 2016, http://europa
.eu/youth/node/32544_en.

5. Sarah Dejaegher, "Europa and the Bull: The Significance of
the Myth in Modern Europe," *New Federalist*, June 13, 2011, accessed
November 2, 2016, http://www.thenewfederalist.eu/Europa-and-the-bull
-The-significance-of-the-myth-in-modern-Europe.

6. Conrad Hackett, "5 Facts About the Muslim Population in Europe,"
Pew Research Center, July 19, 2016, accessed November 2, 2016, http://
www.pewresearch.org/fact-tank/2016/07/19/5-facts-about-the-muslim
-population-in-europe/.

7. David Barrett, "Violent Crime Jumps 27 Per Cent in New Figures
Released by the Office for National Statistics," *Telegraph*, January 22, 2016,
accessed November 2, 2016, http://www.telegraph.co.uk/news/uknews
/crime/12112024/Violent-crime-jumps-27-in-new-figures.html; Soeren Kern,
"Germany: Migrant Rape Crisis Worsens," Gatestone Institute, March 5,
2016, accessed November 2, 2016, https://www.gatestoneinstitute.org/7557
/germany-rape-migrants-crisis.

8. Jonathan Owen, "End of the EU? Germany Warns Five More Countries Could Leave Europe after Brexit," *Express*, June 26, 2016, November 2,
2016, http://www.express.co.uk/news/world/683224/END-OF-THE-EU
-Germany-France-Austria-Hungary-Finland-Netherlands-Europe-Brexit.

9. Jennifer Rankin, et al., "EU Leaders Call for UK to Leave as Soon as Possible," *Guardian*, June 24, 2016, accessed November 2, 2016, https://www.theguardian.com/politics/2016/jun/24/europe-plunged-crisis-britain-votes-leave-eu-european-union; Tim Sculthorpe, "'Vicious' EU Leaders Could 'Lose the Plot' over Brexit, Irish PM Enda Kenny Warns as He Claims Theresa May Could Trigger Negotiations Within Weeks," *Daily Mail*, November 2, 2016, accessed November 2, 2016, http://www.dailymail.co.uk/news/article-3897154/People-able-travel-freely-UK-Ireland-Brexit-Irish-PM-Enda-Kenny-signals.html.

10. Josephus, *Antiquities of the Jews, Book I*, chap. 6, accessed November 3, 2016, http://www.interhack.net/projects/library/antiquities-jews/b1c6.html#pref.

11. Thomas Ice, "Ezekiel 38 & 39 (Part 4)," Pre-Trib Research Center, accessed December 20, 2016, http://www.pre-trib.org/articles/view/ezekiel-38-39-part-4.

12. C. I. Scofield, *Scofield Reference Notes (1917 Edition)*, "Ezekiel 38," Bible Study Tools, accessed November 3, 2016, http://www.biblestudytools.com/commentaries/scofield-reference-notes/ezekiel/ezekiel-38.html.

13. "Meshech," *Holman Bible Dictionary*, StudyLight.org, accessed November 3, 2016, https://www.studylight.org/dictionaries/hbd/view.cgi?number=T4252.

14. "Table: Muslim Population by Country," Pew Research Center, January 27, 2011, accessed November 3, 2016, http://www.pewforum.org/2011/01/27/table-muslim-population-by-country/.

15. "Israel International Relations: Sudan," Jewish Virtual Library, accessed November 3, 2016, https://www.jewishvirtuallibrary.org/jsource/Politics/sudan.html; Mohamed Abdi Farah, "Anti Israel and Ethiopia Protest in Somali Capital," August 11, 2006, accessed November 3, 2016, https://www.somalinet.com/forums/viewtopic.php?t=68389; Preeti Bhattacharji, "State Sponsors: Sudan," Council on Foreign Relations, updated April 2, 2008, accessed November 3, 2016; Bronwyn E. Burton, "Somalia," Council on Foreign Relations, accessed November 3, 2016, http://www.cfr.org/somalia/somalia/p21421.

16. Eric Reeves, "Sudan, Iran, the Obama Administration, and Khartoum's Political Vision," *Sudan Tribune*, October 15, 2014, accessed November 3, 2016, http://www.sudantribune.com/spip.php?article52747.

17. "Al-Shabaab," National Counterterrorism Center, accessed November 3, 2016, https://www.nctc.gov/site/groups/al_shabaab.html.

18. Wikipedia, s.v. "Ethiopia-Israel Relations," accessed December 20, 2016, https://en.wikipedia.org/wiki/Ethiopia%E2%80%93Israel_relations.

19. Maurice Roumani, "The Final Exodus of the Libyan Jews in 1967," Jerusalem Center for Public Affairs, October 28, 2007, accessed November 3, 2016, http://jcpa.org/article/the-final-exodus-of-the-libyan-jews-in-1967/.

20. E. C. Bragg, "Systematic Theology Eschatology Study of Prophecy," Trinity College, accessed November 3, 2016, http://www.trinitycollege.edu /assets/files/ECBragg/ProphecyR.pdf.

21. "Gomer," *Easton's Bible Dictionary*, Bible Hub, accessed November 3, 2016, http://biblehub.com/topical/g/gomer.htm.

22. Fred G. Zaspel, "The Nations of Ezekiel 38–39," Fred Zaspel's Biblical Studies, accessed November 3, 2016, http://www.biblicalstudies.com /bstudy/eschatology/ezekiel.htm.

23. "Erdogan and the Return of the Ottoman Empire," *New Observer*, May 12, 2016, accessed November 3, 2016, http://newobserveronline.com /erdogan-return-ottoman-empire/; Nick Danforth, "Turkey's New Maps Are Reclaiming the Ottoman Empire," *Foreign Policy*, October 23, 2016, accessed December 20, 2016, http://foreignpolicy.com/2016/10/23/turkeys -religious-nationalists-want-ottoman-borders-iraq-erdogan/.

24. "Russia Blocked Israeli Military Fights over Syria, Lebanon," Mint-Press News, October 19, 2015, accessed November 3, 2016, http://www .mintpressnews.com/russia-blocked-israeli-military-fights-over-syria -lebanon/210449/.

25. Jonathan Vankin, "Jewish Theology on Gog & Magog," People of Our Everyday Life, accessed November 3, 2016, http://peopleof.ourevery daylife.com/jewish-theology-gog-magog-9400.html.

26. Chuck Smith, "C2000 Series on Ezekiel 36–39," Blue Letter Bible, accessed November 3, 2016, https://www.blueletterbible.org/Comm/smith _chuck/c2000_Eze/Eze_036.cfm.

27. Edward Wells, *Sacred Geography* (n.p.: Samuel Etheridge, 1817), 20.

28. Isidore Singer, M. Seligsohn, "Tarshish," *Jewish Encyclopedia*, accessed November 3, 2016, http://www.jewishencyclopedia.com/articles /14254-tarshish.

29. J. P. Weethee, *Eastern Question in Its Various Phases* (Whitefish, MT: Kessinger, 2010), 293.

30. See prophecydepotministries.net.

31. Shoebat and Richardson wrote about these groups from a Middle Eastern perspective in their book, *God's War on Terror* (n.p.: Top Executive Media, 2008), 242–43. Bill Salus, however, devotes an entire book to this prophecy in his book *Psalm 83, The Missing Prophecy Revealed: How Israel Becomes the Next Mideast Superpower* (n.p.: Prophecy Depot, 2013).

32. Salus, *Psalm 83*.

33. Bill Salus, "The Two End Time's Judgments Upon Edom—Part One," blog, April 12, 2010, accessed November 3, 2016, http://prophecy depot.blogspot.com/2010/04/two-end-times-judgments-upon-edom-part .html.

34. "Terrorism Havens: Lebanon," Council on Foreign Relations, updated May 1, 2007, accessed November 3, 2016, http://www.cfr.org /lebanon/terrorism-havens-lebanon/p9516.

35. "Takfiri-Salafi Group (Jordan)," TRAC (Terrorism Research & Analysis Consortium), accessed November 3, 2016, http://www.tracking terrorism.org/group/takfiri-salafi-group-jordan.

36. Yaakov Lappin, "Unstable Neighborhood: Terrorist Groups Encircle Israel," Gatestone Institute, February 25, 2014, accessed November 3, 2016, https://www.gatestoneinstitute.org/4191/terrorist-groups-encircle-israel.

37. "Just *Who* Are the 'Palestinians'?" Hope of Israel Ministries, accessed December 20, 2016, http://www.hope-of-israel.org/whopal.html.

38. The children of Lot were Ammon of northern Jordan and Moab of central Jordan.

39. Ryan Browne, "State Department Report Finds Iran Is Top State Sponsor of Terror," CNN, updated June 2, 2016, accessed November 3, 2016, http://www.cnn.com/2016/06/02/politics/state-department-report -terrorism/; Mohamad Bazzi, "Iran Will Do What It Takes to Fight ISIS," CNN, updated January 3, 2015, accessed November 3, 2016, http://www .cnn.com/2015/01/03/opinion/bazzi-iran-iraq/.

40. Riyadh Mohammed, "How Iran Is Taking Over the Middle East," *Fiscal Times*, March 18, 2015, accessed November 3, 2016, http://www .thefiscaltimes.com/2015/03/18/How-Iran-Taking-Over-Middle-East.

41. "Damascus," *New World Encyclopedia*, accessed November 3, 2016, http://www.newworldencyclopedia.org/entry/Damascus#cite_note -Syrian_Population-0.

42. Aaron Klein, "Syria Threatens Israel on Golan Heights," *New York Sun*, July 8, 2007, accessed November 4, 2016, http://www.nysun.com /foreign/syria-threatens-israel-on-golan-heights/58009/; Dov Lieber, "Syria Vows to Use 'Any Means Necessary' to Take Back Golan," *Times of Israel*, April 17, 2016, accessed November 4, 2016, http://www.timesofisrael.com /syria-vows-to-use-any-means-necessary-to-take-back-golan/.

43. Paul Alster, "Potentially Game-Changing Oil Reserves Discovered in Israel," Fox News, October 8, 2015, accessed November 4, 2016, http:// www.foxnews.com/world/2015/10/07/potentially-game-changing-oil -reserves-discovered-in-israel.html.

44. Herb Keinon, "Netanyahu Warns Israel Will Respond 'Fiercely' If It Sees Any Attempt of a Syrian Attack," *Jerusalem Post*, August 27, 2013,

accessed December 20, 2016, http://www.jpost.com/Middle-East
/Netanyahu-warns-Israel-will-respond-fiercely-if-it-sees-any-attempt-of-a
-Syrian-attack-324428.

45. Patrick Goodenough, "Don't Try It, Israel Warns Syria—Amid
Threats From Damascus, Tehran," CNSNews.com, August 28, 2013,
accessed November 4, 2016, http://www.cnsnews.com/news/article/don-t
-try-it-israel-warns-syria-amid-threats-damascus-tehran.

46. Bill Salus, "Elam: Iran's Forgotten Prophecy," Koinonia House,
accessed November 4, 2016, http://khouse.org/articles/2014/1199.

47. Bill Salus, *Nuclear Showdown in Iran: Revealing the Ancient Prophecy
of Elam* (n.p.: Prophecy Depot, 2014).

48. Sarah Stegall, "Evangelists Say Muslims Coming to Christ at Historic Rate," *Charisma*, August 20, 2010, accessed December 20, 2016,
http://www.charismamag.com/site-archives/570-news/featured-news/11719
-evangelists-say-muslims-coming-to-christ-at-historic-rate; Stoyan Zaimov,
"Muslims Tired of Islamic Extremism Turning to Jesus Christ, Message of
Peace, Says CEO of Arabic TV Network," *Christian Post*, March 22, 2016,
accessed December 20, 2016, http://www.christianpost.com/news/isis
-islamic-extremists-muslims-turning-to-jesus-christ-christianity-message
-of-peace-159764/#HJLeg93hsqPA63pp.99.

49. "Visions of Jesus Stir Muslim Hearts," CBN, accessed December 20,
2016, http://www1.cbn.com/onlinediscipleship/visions-of-jesus-stir-muslim
-hearts.

50. Blago Kirov, *Napoleon Bonaparte: Quotes & Facts* (CreateSpace
Independent Publishing Platform, 2015), 22.

51. Hannah Beech, "The World's Next Superpower Announces Itself
With an Epic Parade," *Time*, September 3, 2015, accessed November 4,
2016, http://time.com/4021131/china-parade-beijing-military-world-war/.

52. "Israeli Defence Chief in India to Boost Arms Sales," *National*, February 18, 2015, accessed November 4, 2016, http://www.thenational.ae
/world/middle-east/israeli-defence-chief-in-india-to-boost-arms-sales;
"Overview of India-Israel Bilateral Trade and Economic Relations," Ministry of Economy and Industry, accessed November 4, 2016, http://itrade
.gov.il/india/israel-india/.

53. Herb Keinon, "India Again Abstains in Israel-Related UN Vote,"
Jerusalem Post, July 21, 2015, accessed November 4, 2016, http://www.jpost
.com/International/India-again-abstains-in-Israel-related-UN-vote-409721.

Chapter 7
The United States in Bible Prophecy:
What the Future Holds for This Superpower

1. Joshua J. Mark, "Roman Standard," Ancient History Encyclopedia, accessed November 4, 2016, http://www.ancient.eu/Roman_Standard/.

2. Wikipedia, s. v. "Gallery of Country Coats of Arms," accessed November 4, 2016, https://en.wikipedia.org/wiki/Gallery_of_country _coats_of_arms.

3. Bethany Blankley, "Planned Parenthood's Goddess Projected Onto Empire State Building," Charisma News, August 20, 2015, accessed October 31, 2016, http://www.charismanews.com/opinion/51132-planned -parenthood-s-goddess-projected-onto-empire-state-building.

4. Caitlin Mota, "One World Trade Center Lights Up in Rainbow Colors," NJ.com, June 29, 2015, accessed November 4, 2016, http://www .nj.com/hudson/index.ssf/2015/06/photos_one_world_trade_center _lights_up_in_rainbow.html.

5. Mark Martin, "Rabbi Jonathan Cahn Warns America on Temple of Ba'al," CBN News, September 28, 2016, accessed December 20, 2016, http://www1.cbn.com/cbnnews/us/2016/september/rabbi-jonathan-cahns -warning-for-america-about-nycs-temple-of-baal-arch-replica.

6. Britt Gillette, "America in Bible Prophecy," End Times Bible Prophecy, accessed November 4, 2016, http://www.end-times-bible -prophecy.com/america-in-bible-prophecy.html.

7. Steven Ertelt, "58,586,256 Abortions in America Since Roe v. Wade in 1973," LifeNews.com, January 14, 2016, accessed November 4, 2016, http://www.lifenews.com/2016/01/14/58586256-abortions-in-america-since -roe-v-wade-in-1973/.

8. Benjamin Rush, *The Autobiography of Benjamin Rush*, as quoted in Roger Anghis, "Defining America and America's Exceptionalism, Part 1," NewsWithViews.com, accessed January 12, 2017, http://www.newswith views.com/Anghis/roger162.htm#_ftn5.

9. "Cheney Takes Flamethrower to Obama," Fox News, December 6, 2012, accessed December 20, 2016, http://nation.foxnews.com/dick-cheney /2012/12/06/cheney-takes-flamethrower-obama.

10. "Trump Vows to 'Rebuild' Military, in American Legion Address," FOX News, September 1, 2016, accessed December 20, 2016, http://www .foxnews.com/politics/2016/09/01/trump-vows-to-rebuild-military-in -american-legion-address.html.

11. John Sullivan and Justin Johnson, "America's Military Is in Much Worse Shape Than You'd Think," Daily Signal, March 25, 2016, accessed

December 20, 2016, http://dailysignal.com/2016/03/25/americas-military-is
-in-much-worse-shape-than-youd-think.

12. "Interest Expense on the Debt Outstanding," accessed December 20, 2016, https://www.treasurydirect.gov/govt/reports/ir/ir_expense.htm.

13. Global Debt Enters Terminal Velocity Mode: Why Central Banks Have No Intention of Slowing Their Public and Private Debt Binge," My Budget 360, accessed December 20, 2016, http://www.mybudget360.com /global-debt-total-central-bank-balance-sheet-expansion-debt/.

14. "Exporting America," CNN, accessed January 1, 2017, http://www .cnn.com/CNN/Programs/lou.dobbs.tonight/popups/exporting.america /frameset.exclude.html.

15. George Washington, "Farewell Address," September 19, 1796, The Heritage Foundation, accessed November 4, 2016, http://www.heritage .org/initiatives/first-principles/primary-sources/washingtons-farewell -address.

16. "Convergence: What Does It All Mean?," Olive Tree Ministries, August 29, 2015, accessed November 4, 2016, http://www.olivetreeviews .org/radio/complete-archives?start=110.

Chapter 8
The Mystery Nation: You Carry the Power of Another World

1. Blue Letter Bible, s.v. "*mystērion*," accessed November 7, 2016, https:// www.blueletterbible.org/lang/lexicon/lexicon.cfm?Strongs=G3466&t =KJV.

2. Charles Chandler, "Revival Breaks Out in West Virginia," Billy Graham Evangelistic Association, May 29, 2016, accessed November 7, 2016, https://billygraham.org/decision-magazine/june-2016/revival-breaks -out-in-west-virginia/.

3. Cornelius Quek, "Azusa Now What? Prophetic Perspectives on the Imminent Move of God," Charisma News, April 13, 2016. Accessed November 7, 2016, http://www.charismanews.com/opinion/56442-azusa -now-what-prophetic-perspectives-on-the-imminent-move-of-god.

4. Blue Letter Bible, s.v. "*elpis*," accessed November 7, 2016, https:// www.blueletterbible.org/lang/lexicon/lexicon.cfm?Strongs=G1680&t =KJV.

5. Peter Kuzmic's Twitter page, June 3, 2015, accessed November 7, 2016, https://twitter.com/peterkuzmic/status/606024453756198912.

6. Andrew Murray, "15 Famous Quotes and 5 Principles About Prayer," iPost, accessed November 7, 2016, http://ipost.christianpost.com/post/15 -famous-quotes-and-5-principles-about-prayer.

7. *Second Shift: From Crisis to Collaboration*, accessed November 7, 2016, http://www.secondshiftfilm.com/.

Chapter 9
The Great Secret Revealed: The Mystery of the Disappearance of Millions

1. Traditionally attributed to Mark Twain, "How Mark Twain Really Felt About Cincinnati," Cincinnati.com, April 13, 2016, accessed November 7, 2016, http://www.cincinnati.com/story/news/history/2016/02/18 /adventures-huck-finn-published-today-1885/80545822/.

2. "What Did Ancient Church Fathers Believe About the Rapture?," Beginning and End, August 2, 2013, accessed November 7, 2016, http:// beginningandend.com/what-did-ancient-church-fathers-believe-about-the -rapture/.

3. Keith A. Sherlin, "The History of the Pre-trib Rapture," Essential Christianity, accessed November 7, 2016, http://www.essentialchristianity .com/pages.asp?pageid=21918.

4. Chuck Missler, "Byzantine Text Discovery: Ephraem the Syrian," Koinonia House, accessed November 7, 2016, http://khouse.org/articles /1995/39/.

5. Blue Letter Bible, s.v. "*ek*," accessed November 7, 2016, https://www .blueletterbible.org/lang/lexicon/lexicon.cfm?Strongs=G1537&t=KJV.

Chapter 10
The Final *Shabua*: Earth's Inescapable Hour of Agony and Distress

1. "Sweden Close to Being a Cashless Society," The Local, October 12, 2014, accessed November 8, 2016, http://www.thelocal.se/20141012/sweden -close-to-being-cashless-society-report.

2. "MasterCard Tracks Global 'Cashless Journey,'" Finextra, September 23, 2013, accessed November 8, 2016, https://www.finextra.com/news /announcement.aspx?pressreleaseid=51842&topic=stp.

3. David Lev, "Will Israel Be the World's First 'No Cash' Society?," Arutz Sheva, September 17, 2013, accessed November 8, 2016, http://www .israelnationalnews.com/News/News.aspx/172028.

4. Daniel 11:24 is a reference to Antiochus Epiphanes, a type of the coming Antichrist. See also http://www.prophecyforum.com/antiochus .html.

5. Steven Ertelt, "58,586,256 Abortions in America Since Roe v. Wade in 1973," LifeNews.com, January 14, 2016, accessed November 4, 2016, http://www.lifenews.com/2016/01/14/58586256-abortions-in-america-since -roe-v-wade-in-1973/.

6. Adapted from my sermon, May 12, 1985, Mount Hope Church in Lansing, Michigan, inspired by the late Dr. Glen Cole and Pastor Tommy Barnett.

Chapter 11
The Coming Kingdom: After Jesus Returns

1. One thousand two hundred sixty days from the time the Antichrist moves his image into the temple, Jesus will return to earth (Dan. 12:7). A "time, times, and half a time" is three and a half years. Since the Book of Revelation reverts to Hebrew terminology beginning in chapter 6, a year is 360 days. (See also Revelation 12:6, 14; 11:3; 13:5.) Forty-two months, 1,260 days, and "time, times, and half a time" refer to the same time period. Thirty additional days will be necessary to clean up all Antichrist images and other references around the planet, making it 1,290 days (Dan. 12:11). Then, 45 days of judging the nations for how they treated Israel, brings it to 1,335 days (Dan. 12:12).

Chapter 12
Final Words: Admonitions and Encouragement

1. "Historic First: Islamic Prayers Held at the Vatican," CBN News, September 8, 2014, accessed November 8, 2016, http://www1.cbn.com/cbn news/world/2014/June/Historic-First-Islamic-Prayers-Held-at-the-Vatican.

2. Shelley Klein, *The Most Evil Dictators in History* (London: Michael O'Mara Books, 2004).

BIBLIOGRAPHY

Ahn, Ché. *Say Goodbye to Powerless Christianity: Walking in Supernatural Surrender and Significance*. Shippensburg, PA: Destiny Image, 2009.

Block, Daniel. *The Book of Ezekiel, Chapters 25–48*. NICOT. Grand Rapids: Eerdmans, 1998.

Boyd, Frank M. *Prophetic Light*. Springfield, MO: Gospel Publishing House, 1968.

Cahn, Jonathan. *The Harbinger: The Ancient Mystery that Holds the Secret of America's Future*. Lake Mary, FL: FrontLine, 2012.

Cantelon, Willard. *The Day the Dollar Dies*. Alachua, FL: Bridge-Logos, 2009.

Geisler, Norman. *Systematic Theology*. Minneapolis: Bethany House, 2005.

Hindson, Ed. *Approaching Armageddon*. Eugene, OR: Harvest House, 1975.

———. *Final Signs*. Eugene, OR: Harvest House, 1996.

Hitchcock, Mark. *Bible Prophecy*. Wheaton, IL: Tyndale House, 1999.

———. *Is America in Bible Prophecy?* Sisters, OR: Multnomah, 2002.

———. *The Second Coming of Babylon*. Sisters, OR: Multnomah, 2003.

Hodge, Charles. *Systematic Theology*. Grand Rapids: Eerdmans, 1952.

Ice, Thomas, and Timothy Demy. *Prophecy Watch*. Eugene, OR: Harvest House, 1998.

Ice, Thomas, and Randall Price. *Ready to Rebuild: The Imminent Plan to Rebuild the Last Days Temple*. Eugene, OR: Harvest House, 1992.

Jeffrey, Grant R. *One Nation, Under Attack: How Big-Government Liberals Are Destroying the America You Love*. Colorado Springs: WaterBrook, 2012.

Koenig, William R. *Eye to Eye: Facing the Consequences of Dividing Israel*. McLean, VA: About Him, 2008.

LaHaye, Tim, and Ed Hindson. *The Popular Bible Prophecy Commentary*. Eugene, OR: Harvest House, 2006.

Missler, Chuck. *The Rapture*. Couer d'Alene, ID: Koinonia House, 2014.

Pentecost, J. Dwight. *Things to Come*. Grand Rapids: Zondervan, 1964.

Prince, Derek. *Prophetic Guide to the End Times*. Grand Rapids: Chosen, 2008.

Reagan, David R. *America the Beautiful? The United States in Bible Prophecy*. McKinney, TX: Lamb & Lion Ministries, 2003.

Rhodes, Ron. *Christ Before the Manger: The Life and Times of The Pre-Incarnate Christ*. Grand Rapids: Baker, 1992.

———. *The End Times in Chronological Order*. Eugene, OR: Harvest House, 2012.

———. *The Popular Dictionary of Bible Prophecy*. Eugene, OR: Harvest House, 2010.

Rosenberg, Joel. *Epicenter: Why Current Rumblings in the Middle East Will Change Your Future*. Carol Stream, IL: Tyndale House, 2006.

Salus, Bill. *Nuclear Showdown in Iran: The Ancient Prophecy of Elam*. La Quinta, CA: Prophecy Depot, 2014.

———. *Psalm 83, The Missing Prophecy Revealed: How Israel Becomes the Next Mideast Superpower*. La Quinta, CA: Prophecy Depot, 2013.

Thomas, F. W. *Masters of Deception*. Grand Rapids: Baker, 1983.

Van Impe, Jack. *Coming Soon: Earth's Golden Age*. Troy, MI: JVIM Books, 2008.

———. *Final Mysteries Unsealed*. Troy, MI: JVIM Books, 1998.

———. *Israel's Final Holocaust*. Troy, MI: JVIM Books, 1979.

Walvoord, John F. *End Times*. Nashville: Word, 1998.

———. *The Millennial Kingdom*. Grand Rapids: Zondervan, 1975.

Williams, Dave. *End Times Prophecy*. Lansing, MI: MHC Books, 1991.

———. *Skill for Battle*. Lansing, MI: Decapolis, 2009.

———. *What to Do If You Miss the Rapture*. Lansing, MI: Decapolis, 1998.

———. *The World Beyond*. Lansing, MI: Decapolis, 2002.

Contact Information

Dave Williams Ministries
P.O. Box 80825
Lansing, MI 48908-0825

For a complete list of Dave Williams'
life-changing books, audio messages,
and videos visit our website:
DaveWilliams.com

or phone:
800-888-7284 or 517-731-0000

**"Understand Biblical
Prophecies Coming
True In our Day"**
Get a free audio download
at: **DaveWilliams.com/ET**

CONNECT WITH US!